# The Music Therapy Profession

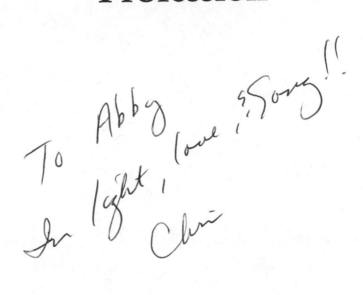

To Abby
In light, love, § Song!!
Chris

# The Music Therapy Profession

*Inspiring Health, Wellness, and Joy*

**Christine Korb**

**To order additional copies of this book, contact:**
Xlibris
1-888-795-4274
www.Xlibris.com
Orders@Xlibris.com
550790

# Contents

Preface ..................................................................................9

Chapter 1: Who Are Music Therapists?........................................... 19

Chapter 2: Finding a Music Therapy Program ...............................34

Chapter 3: Admission to a Music Therapy Program .......................37

Chapter 4: Where Do Music Therapists Work?..............................73

Chapter 5: What Is a Typical Music Therapy Session? .................. 117

Chapter 6: Music Therapy Practice Internationally .....................123

Chapter 7: What Is the Future of Music Therapy?.........................125

Notes ................................................................................129

Further Resources ............................................................. 131

About the Author ............................................................. 133

# Acknowledgments

Encounters with music therapists and prospective music therapy students over the past twenty-six years have enormously contributed to the seed development, gestation period, and final birthing of this book. Many of those remarkable students from Marylhurst University have now become colleagues and friends. To all of you I send my deepest gratitude and blessings.

My deepest thanks to Betsey Carle, colleague, friend, and the first Marylhurst University student who supported my journey and this book during some important days of transition.

An abundance of thanks to my editor, Lori Stephens, Verbatim Editorial LLC, who stepped in at the last minute to lend her expertise and to help finalize this project, and to Rey Santos, consultant with XLibris, for his gentle nudging over the past months.

I also give thanks to the many colleagues over the years and across the country who have helped me become the music therapist and educator I am today. In particular I would like to thank Dr. Kate Gfeller, Dr. William Davis, and Dr. Michael Thaut with whom I studied while pursuing my music therapy degree at Colorado State University. Their inspiration has been a powerful influence in my music therapy journey.

I'm also grateful for the musical training in performance and composition I received from Dr. James McCray, Dr. Janet Landreth, and Patricia Burge while studying at Colorado State University. Their mentoring voices continue to inspire me in the quiet of the night.

I would especially like to thank Jodi Winnwalker, CEO of Earthtones Music Therapy Services, my first faculty colleague and my first Oregonian friend.

I give special thanks to Dr. Jane Andrews, Dr. Carlene Brown, Jane Creagan, Maureen Hearns, Lalene Kay, and Dr. Barbara Wheeler, and

Dr. Beth York for their safety net of encouragement and supportive friendship over the years. I would like to give special thanks to Peter Zisa—colleague, friend, and my brother in music for his support and gentle kindness over the years.

Special thanks to Ebe McAuliffe, Maria Olaya, and Rebbecca Vickerman for the generosity of their time and assistance during the writing process.

I would like to thank my daughters, Tracy and Amy, for their highly spirited and talented friendship over the years. One mother should be so lucky! I especially thank psychotherapist, colleague, and dear friend Darilou Potter, whose unwavering and creative friendship helped galvanize my direction as a music therapist and educator.

I owe much gratitude to Dr. Greg Steinke, who first believed in my abilities to create and develop a music therapy program of quality and lasting influence at Marylhurst University.

Lastly, I would like to thank Pacific University and its kind and talented faculty. I am grateful to be its director of music therapy and to help launch its music therapy program.

# Preface

This is not an ordinary book about music therapy. It is not a "how to use music to heal" manual for individuals seeking to enhance their own therapeutic skills by using music. In the past fifteen to twenty years, the popular press has exploded with material about the healing powers of music and how one can use music as therapy—which is not music therapy. (See www.musictherapy.org.)

I would like to present for your heartfelt consideration the answer to the question, "What is music therapy?" through my experiences and, most importantly, through the fresh eyes of the students I have been privileged to teach over the years. These students have now become valued colleagues.

This is a book about the soul and spirit of the music therapist and what drives the prospective student to seriously consider the profession, because it is one of the newest and yet oldest of all the healing professions. This book is also for the working musician who is curious about the profession of music therapy.

How can the musician make a difference? In what way can the musician make a living and make a difference? What is the soul of the musician or music therapist? Why music therapy? As Jessica Western says in the postscript to her essay, "In doing this work, I feel in alignment with my highest potentials as a musician, as a therapist, and as a human being."

What a joy to witness the journey of students, now colleagues, who have come to the shores of this healing profession. In moments of reflection, I've allowed myself to look back on my own journey, which has included the most precious clients and patients I could ever imagine working with. Subsequently, my work has included serving as teacher and mentor to some of the most incredible, idealistic, and talented music therapy students to grace an educator's classroom. I have been honored to serve as their advisor, teacher, supervisor, and colleague.

## Student Essays

I have included the audition essays that students write to enter a music therapy program. These essays describe the personal reasons for entering a music therapy program. They also share some common threads as evidenced in the headings under which they are presented. What a joy it has been to witness the journeys of these colleagues! My appreciation for everyone I have had the privilege of mentoring and advising over the past fourteen years is beyond words.

Some essays are not included only because of availability, connecting with and contacting colleagues, and timing for the first edition of this book.

## My Journey

The music calling has been with me since I was young.

It all began while singing the Latin responses of the Catholic rituals. I participated in high school musicals and choirs with a gaggle of gifted friends. I saw my parents, aunts, and uncles gather around the piano during family holidays, joyfully singing their favorite songs of the day. These included refrains from musicals, gospels, and songs known by heart.

All the while, I was taking to heart the intuitive power of every strain one could imagine. Classical, popular, folk, some of the rich musical scores of Rodgers and Hammerstein, and a plethora of jazz standards contributed to my love affair with music. I did not know about music therapy until well past the time to declare a major in college.

Driven by an innate passion to help others, and coming of age during one of the most tumultuous times in our country's history (the

1960s), I transferred my pianistic pursuits to the guitar. I said, "You can't carry a piano on your back like you can a guitar." I began to make my way as a folk musician, teaching friends and young students my elemental guitar savvy while harboring the idealism and spiritual torment of those days.

I purchased one guitar after another, all the while chasing the "perfect sound" and the perfect playability. No one ever told me that the "action" of a guitar could be lowered. I was constantly looking for that one perfect instrument whose strings were the perfect distance from the fret board! I taught others what I knew as I learned, wanting to share the perfect voice sounding from the ribs and body of that perfect guitar. This was my wonderful life in Colorado as a wife and mother to two lovely, precocious, and gifted daughters!

I exploded into adulthood in the 1970s with my guitar and daughters in hand, and I achieved just enough success as a singer-songwriter to be coaxed into entertaining. I took a road trip with a small band of working musicians, recorded original songs with new friends, and volunteered as a church musician. These experiences highlighted my days of self-directed music training. Add to this the formation of a folk group of guitarists, banjo players, and a gutbucket player. We made music in our living rooms and around the campfire. Life was a rich and full experience!

The spirit began gently tugging at my soul. Music's voice was changing her timbre, and I listened. I wasn't sure where the muse of music was taking me, but something was changing deep inside.

I began to volunteer at music sing-alongs at older adult and assisted living homes. I was intrigued with the residents' responses to singing traditional tunes like "Home on the Range," "I've Been Working on the Railroad," and "Down by the Riverside." I felt the atmosphere change as we sang together. I did not provide the residents with any instruments—it was more of a performance in hopes of enticing them to sing with me as their leader.

Fast forward to the 1980s, and music's soulful tug began to entice me in a new direction. I studied jazz piano and met musical mentors at the college level. How exciting it was to be learning a new musical voice: jazz and improvisation! Following a year of study, I returned to school to study music and become a "legit" musician. I was inspired by a host of young musicians, and I began awakening to the professional side of a musician's journey.

I began my studies as a composition major, added music education and music therapy training, and earned a graduate degree in music therapy. During this time, I continued teaching guitar and piano in my home studio while balancing a satisfying life as a mother, wife, and music student.

After a percussion jury, my technique teacher asked, "Chris, why weren't you here twenty years ago?" I pondered the comment for a long time. I know I wouldn't have had the variety of rich life experiences that I did if music had been my first profession. There are no mistakes in timing!

## Why Music Therapy, and Why Now?

There is an awakening today because of the energetics of our age—a convergence of the energies of the scientific age and the age of the spirit. An intuitional guidance system is beginning to take center stage in the lives of awakening spirits. Spiritual teachers such as Sonja Grace, Carolyn Myss, Marianne Williamson, Pema Chodron, the Dalai Lama, Ram Dass, Wayne Dyer, and Jon Cabot-Zinn are calling out the Spirit to help those in need of guidance.

Who do musicians turn to? This is an individual preference. It all depends on who we like to listen to and who inspires us during our development. Being exposed to music masters such as Bach, Brahms, Chopin, Debussy, Hildegard of Bingen and more contemporary composers such as Aaron Copeland, Ennio Morricone, John Cage, Bobby McFerrin, The Beatles, U2, Carole King, Joan Baez, Joni Mitchell, and James Taylor inspire us to think of making music in some capacity. How many of us can make an adequate living on the "big stage," however that stage may be interpreted?

In this one life we have, many of us are filled with the desire to make a difference in the lives of others through music. The desire to make a difference in the lives of others while also using one's musical gifts gradually becomes stronger than performing for performance's sake. Stepping off the center stage and replacing it with another's needs calls the young, or young at heart, music maker to the profession of music therapy.

Music therapy is a calling of the soul's deepest longing. It includes all the requirements needed to become clinically proficient for the profession, it enables us to work with the most fragile and challenged people, and it combines the musician's toolbox of musical gifts. Rather than tickling the ears as a performer, music therapists seek the deeper, more soul-satisfying relationships that can occur in a one-on-one setting or in small groups. To create an environment for change or to support or improve physical, emotional, or social functioning are some of the motivations that drive the heart and soul of a music therapist.

## Questions about Music

There always seem to be more questions about music than we have answers for. Jake Beck amplifies some of those questions (see his complete essay at the end of this chapter). He asks the following:

Is music the most purely emotional of all arts and sciences? Can it be studied scientifically? Quantifiably? Can it be used specifically to alter or service emotion? Does music enhance cognizance in children, the mentally ill, and the elderly? Is it effective in this way? Why are some autistic people incredibly and indelibly gifted musically? Is music an effective communicator between people where no other communication suffices? Is it truly the universal language?

These are a few of the questions that I've heard from students who are curious about music therapy. The search for the answers often draws them into a music therapy program.

## Overview

The chapters will help the student of music, professional musician, or music lover understand what motivates the prospective music therapy student. I believe it is a calling of the Spirit, sounded by the soul's lament, to become more and to become embodied within the human spirit.

Chapter 1 includes answers to the questions so often asked of the music therapist: who are we, why we have come to music therapy, and what do we do. Chapter 2 describes the "what," how we receive the training to become a music therapist, which schools offer music therapy programs, and the background or experience necessary to enroll in a music therapy program. The admission process to a music therapy program is discussed in Chapter 3, and the chapter also includes the essential skills necessary for those who are interested in becoming a music therapist. Chapter 4 discusses the sites where a music therapist may be employed (the "where" of employment). Chapter 5 details several scenarios of a music therapy session and the questions that are often asked about what we do and how we do it. Chapter 6 acknowledges the world community of music therapy and the state of the profession around the globe. Chapter 7 is a recap of why music therapists are necessary and the need to increase our presence in the United States and around the world.

The essays were written by former students as part of the audition requirements for a music therapy program (all the students are now practicing music therapy around the country and overseas). They write about their feelings and thoughts as they began their journey. The footnotes to the essays describe where they now find themselves, professionally and philosophically, within the profession of music therapy.

I hope you enjoy reading about the why, what, where, and how of music therapy. If you are considering a college degree, are a seasoned working musician, want to change careers, or are curious about the field, perhaps you will consider becoming part of this healing profession. The rewards of the work are well beyond description.

# Essay

## Drawing a Desire to Become a Music Therapist
## H. Jacob Beck, MT-BC

My desire to pursue music therapy is borne of a number of smaller desires and bits of knowledge, each very fundamental: a dedication to music, a dedication to music as being important and ultimately relevant, a growing dedication to people, and my longing to help and coexist.

These and other basic, intuitive wishes make the general foundations of my initial itch to pursue music therapy, but the fleshed out, actual conversation with myself about it always starts and ends with questions. How is music important? Why is it so well represented in nearly all cultures and civilizations? How does it speak to nearly everyone? Why does it cause incredible joy, sorrow, ecstasy, and anger? Is music the most purely emotional of all arts and sciences? Can it be studied scientifically? Quantifiably? Can it be used specifically to alter or service emotion? Does music enhance cognizance in children, the mentally ill, and the elderly? Is it effective in this way? Why are some autistic people incredibly and indelibly gifted musically? Is music an effective communicator between people where no other communication suffices? Is it truly the universal language?

Perhaps some of this thought process is necessarily left unanswered or at least unrequited. I won't pretend to think that the music therapist knows the meaning of life in regard to music any more than an involved composer or an elementary school band instructor. But it seems that the music therapist is different, because they are in communion and working for individuals and groups who are open to and in need of music's most basic principles. There exists in music an emotional relationship with all people, and I think in that relationship is the power to heal and to understand how to heal. No one needs a degree to play a CD, but we do need the clinical training to be in a relationship of music and the heart. The cultural saturation and necessity of music may be evident to me, but I am only on the cusp of understanding how and why a particular piece or song (of any genre or time period) has the incredible power to dictate mood and emotional state. I've played guitar for almost ten years now and have played for many people (friends, family, etc.) in an open or community atmosphere and have felt myself pulling the emotional weight of the gathering with every new song or shifting musical nuance. It is a feeling that satisfies me but which seems almost out of my control—that is, intentionally playing to what I perceive to be the general feeling of a person works only sometimes, and rarely. I feel the musical therapist must know better the mood of the person or patient, or at the very least knows better how to realize, encourage, or remedy that mood, which can be extremely central to overall healthy and healing. I have a tremendous respect for music's empathetic and sympathetic powers but a scant and amateur understanding of them. I know there is a brilliant, graceful, and emotional core to music, and I would like an opportunity to get closer to it.

In regard to myself and looking inward, I have many questions, too, although none carry such importance. How do I utilize my talent as a musician? How can I remain humble and modest with my musical gifts? How can I make music for other people? How do I realize my concern for people's health, mentally or otherwise? How can I help? Can I blend this with a passion for making and knowing music?

All of this suggests to me that I'm again in a place where I am on the edge of beginning to understand but am just a little too far from the core. Since graduating from college with a BA in music, I have been attempting a strange balance: that of keeping immersed in music (through meaningful practice and audio recording) but at the same time pushing it aside so that I could and can remain open to other possibilities in the world, namely those of simple living and self-sufficiency. In some ways, I find a professional music career inherently selfish. I have instead spent my "work" time on an organic farm, passing the time with menial jobs, and the search for other meaning through reading: my "free" time has been taken with making music and replaying it endlessly in my immediate consciousness. I've created an environment where I'm both accepting and denying my musicality. Basically, I've been attempting to create a method of balancing practicality (how to live and support?), compassion (how can I live right, knowing I've contributed something real and loving?), and the surprising realization that I can't just set music aside as unimportant, or worse, as a "hobby"—in ways it is my truest talent and longing to be side by side with it ("The call of the Spirit and the lament of the soul"). The primary reason, then, that I am drawn to music therapy as a career and life choice is that there is the potential in it to satisfy all of the above interests and considerations. I could live with compassion and without guilt in music. I believe that, potentially, music therapy may shed light on many of my questions, big and small, while reinforcing crucial and firmly held personal ideals.

*Jake Beck is now employed with Fort Vancouver Convalescent Center in Vancouver, Washington.*

# Chapter 1: Who Are Music Therapists?

There are many definitions of music therapy. I often describe it as the quintessential marriage of music as art and music as science, thus honoring the art of music along with the scientific implications of the profession. Another one of my favorites is that music therapy is an established healthcare profession that uses the art of music to accomplish nonmusical goals.

In a typical session, the client and therapist may create engagement through musical experiences such as singing, vocalizing, small rhythm instruments or instrument play, movement to music, and songwriting. These experiences may be focused on speech, occupational, physical, academic, and/or behavioral goals. Clients do not need any musical skill or experience to participate in and benefit from music therapy.

Music therapists will take into consideration who we are talking to when providing a definition of music therapy. For example, to the curious checker in the grocery store, it might be best to simply say, "As a music therapist, we use music in a specific way to increase quality of life." In speaking with medical personnel, we would use more sophisticated terms to define music therapy. In answering that question, we are charged with finding creative ways to describe and define our work.

## Where Do Music Therapists Come From?

Music therapists come from everywhere. We each have a style that emerges from our philosophy for practicing work that focuses on another rather than the performer. This is what inspires us to study music therapy in the first place: the desire to point the spotlight on the "other."

In some real respects, the music therapist is always "performing," so performance *skills* are a necessary ingredient as well as using music to improve and uplift the lives of others.

Because we are small in numbers (only around six thousand of us practice in the United States and around eighteen thousand worldwide), it is no wonder that we are sparsely known. One well-known public figure, Senator Gabby Gifford, recently brought the spotlight on music therapy. Her life was in the balance after she was shot in the head at a public forum in Tucson, Arizona, and she received music therapy services during her rehabilitation and recovery. Although the media covered her therapy, it was astonishing that many people did not know that music therapists existed as viable and important members of the health professions!

Some of us come to study music therapy from other professions such as social work, sociology, or psychology. Some might be picking themselves up from the disappointment of marginal success as the singer-songwriter they had hoped to become—record and publishing contracts in hand. They stumble upon a profession that they have never heard of: music therapy! Imagine that—a college degree major that leads to real employment! Why hadn't they thought of that before? What has kept this profession such a secret?

We come from the pool and barroom halls. We come from the disillusionment of the singer-songwriters' paradise, because we're tired of the focus on the music and being able to perform flawlessly for a fickle public. Sometimes we come from the lonely space between the question of "what do I do with my life?" and the notion that "music is all there is." To love and be enchanted by music for music's sake is no longer enough.

Eric Hickey states in his essay:

Over time, something inside of me began to change, and music was something I could no longer confine to the borders of a band, a record label, or an industry. While composing, recording, and performing is something I intend to do for the rest of my life, it is no longer an end in and of itself. I have great curiosity as to the science behind music: what exactly is happening in the brain when music is absorbed and expressed and what healing secrets are hidden in these innate and ancient responses?

We also come to the field as teachers. Letha Winger, a former piano teacher, voiced in her essay, "What I love most about teaching is the way it helps students express their feelings...I love having them feel better when they walk out of my home...I want to be a builder of self-esteem, a bringer of laughter, fun, and joy." Following a lecture and relaxation exercise to Barber's "Adagio for Strings," she said, "My feelings were so powerful that I didn't quite know what to make of it. I only knew that I wished to do something with music and medicine."

We might stumble upon this thing called music therapy and wish to find out more about the field. Who are music therapists? Where do they work? Can I meet one? Is there one in my city? (My dream is that every music therapist has a presence in the media, a column in the newspaper, or an "in the news" spot on television broadcasts.) These are some of the questions asked by people who are casting around for a way to make life work while following an elusive musical muse.

Consider the following statement from Liska McNally, MT-BC, about the desire to become a music therapist:

Many of us who choose to become music therapists are called to the vocation. (I feel this is one aspect that separates us from many other career choice paths—it takes a calling to do this!) Therefore, the very act of becoming a music therapist is the reward itself. It is a transformational process that integrates all of our parts. It is a synthesis of values, skills, passions, and longings. We may choose to seek additional training in other areas that are complementary and allow us to earn a steady income and a socially recognized status, but even then we approach our professions with something unique that can only come from being a music therapist—from undertaking the rigorous study of how music affects and transforms all human processes and in so doing being transformed ourselves.

Such is the sentiment from one who entered a music therapy program and is now the supervisor and owner of Meadowlark Music Therapy Services.

# Essays

## Music Therapy Audition Essay
## Eric Hickey, MT-BC

For as long as I can remember, I have felt guided by music and empowered by the sense of freedom and self-confidence that it brings to my everyday life. After graduating from Kenyon College in 2003, I knew that music was going to be central to the direction my life would take, though at the time I was focused mainly on composition and performance. I believe that the decision to pursue a career in music therapy does not altogether erase these aspirations but causes them to expand and grow into something deeper. Life lessons and work experiences over the past three years have helped me understand what I want, and with this degree of clarity has come a deep-seeded desire to, for lack of a better phrase, do good in this world. Although attending Quaker school from kindergarten through twelfth grade left me no stranger to the notion of helping others, before discovering music therapy, I was struggling to reconcile this social responsibility with a career still focused around music.

In 2004, I accepted a position as program director for a nonprofit martial arts school in South Philadelphia called Zhang Sah (Korean for "brave scholar"). The mission of the school is to use martial arts training to "build excellence of character" in the children by instilling the traditional martial arts tenets of discipline, perseverance, courtesy, respect, and humility into their everyday lives. Many of the children in this program come from broken homes, and the structure and moral guidance provided by the Zhang Sah staff is the most consistent and organized part of their lives.

In October of 2005, I pursued a grant from the Southeastern Philadelphia Collaborative Youth Fund to start a music program with the children that would explore a synthesis between West African drumming and Korean martial arts. While I had only been studying martial arts for one year at the time I received the grant, I had been studying the philosophy and performance of West African drumming for nearly three years. Through drumming, the new group focused on providing all participants with what master Ewe drummer C. K. Ladzekpo calls "a moral consciousness of what is real and important in life and how life ought to be lived." In other words, the program sought to utilize music to reinforce the schools mission to develop character in the children.

In promoting music as an integrated part of the children's everyday lives, I was given daily reminders of the parallels between musical lessons and life lessons. By deconstructing their view of music as a special "talent" held by a "gifted" few, the children were able to accept that each of them had a musical voice of their own. I soon observed how getting a simple technique right, or recognizing a polyrhythm between their part and someone else's, could make the hyper children focus, the shy ones open up, and the uninterested children become totally absorbed with what they were doing. Learning the importance of contributing to an ensemble, accepting the responsibility of remembering parts, and trying to actively listen and creatively respond to what was being played had helped the children become committed, confident and aware members of the Zhang Sah community. It was exciting to observe them carrying this discipline, focus, and enthusiasm into their non-drumming activities.

Unfortunately, my other obligations as program director took me away from the music program, and I eventually resigned from my position at the school to become a probation officer for the city of Philadelphia. I have been in this department for about one year now and have accepted that trying to affect positive change through a field unrelated to music is unnatural for me and therefore less "effective."

Perhaps the most powerful experience that directly inspired my interest in music therapy came several months later when I was visiting my girlfriend's sick grandmother in Canton, Ohio. Over the four years that Abby and I were together, I had spent time with her grandmother (who I knew as Gram Famm due to the last name Fammartino) as a healthy woman on a number of occasions. I had always been struck by how lucid, mentally quick, and physically self-sufficient she was even into her eighties. On this visit, however, a brain tumor had grown too large to remove, and we were making the trip to say our last goodbye. When we arrived, Gramm was terribly uncomfortable, and the doctor said that the tumor was growing so rapidly that she could actually feel the pressure in her head, causing waves of almost unbearable pain. After being in the room for about half an hour, Abby's mother turned to me and asked if I had brought my guitar. When I said that I had, she asked me whether I would mind playing something for Gramm to try to take her mind (and theirs) off of the pain. I had already heard of music therapy at this point but was still shaken by the prospect of bringing music into the room.

Gramm, who was Spanish, had spent her early childhood in Spain and returned to visit regularly throughout her life. She was a huge fan of flamenco music. For my senior recital, I had performed a Hector Villa-Lobos etude that had a flamenco sound to it, and I felt that this was the only piece I could play whose hauntingly redemptive harmonies would neither mock nor manufacture the mood of the room.

When I started to play, Gramm began to moan and cry, mumbling something in Spanish that I couldn't understand. My instinct was to stop, but everyone signaled for me to keep playing, so I did. Through her tears, she intermittently called out for me to speed up or slow down or to play harder or more gently. By the end of the short piece, there was a sense of peace about the room, and Gramm lay there, awake and silent, for several moments before falling asleep. It was the first time I had ever felt anything like that while playing music. To witness how the sound of the instrument reached this woman and brought her to tears—how the melody had exhausted her pain—was an overwhelming affirmation of the boundless potential for music to heal and soothe.

Over time, something inside of me began to change, and music was something I could no longer confine to the borders of a band, a record label, or an industry. While composing, recording, and performing is something I intend to do for the rest of my life, it is no longer an end in and of itself. I have great curiosity as to the science behind music: what exactly is happening in the brain when music is absorbed and expressed and what healing secrets are hidden in these innate and ancient responses? As a music therapist, I have an interest in working with people of all ages who are in hospice care. A fear of death burdens some people for their entire lives, and I anticipate learning new ways of using music to help those nearing their death meet this end with a sense of tranquility. I am also fascinated with the ability of music therapy to help those with Alzheimer's disease recall memories believed to have long since been destroyed, and though my knowledge of this area of research is minimal, I am excited to learn more. With so much time and money dedicated to prolonging human life, I see the task of giving the victims of Alzheimer's a renewed sense of self-worth. As well as bringing some hope and relief to grief-stricken family members, as one of the most medically and morally urgent challenges facing the healthcare profession today.

After corresponding with several people at the university, I have a strong sense that Marylhurst and the surrounding area will provide the resources, atmosphere, and experience needed to help me learn to use music as a tool for healing. It is for this reason that I want to take my first step toward a career in music therapy by earning my degree from the university, so that I may soon become a certified, practicing music therapist.

*Eric Hickey is now employed by Cedar Hills Hospital in Portland, Oregon.*

## Music Therapy Essay
## Liska McNally, MT-BC

Almost every day when my husband, Jon, arrives home from work, he and I engage in an unplanned ritual of singing and chanting together as we go about our evening chores. The songs and chants are emergent, improvisational ditties, shaped around the rhythms of our movements. Sometimes we use words, sometimes not. Sometimes the sounds are slow and plaintive, but more often they are exuberant and silly. This is our way of bonding—of creating the balance needed to live together respectfully. Most of all, it is our way of celebrating the synergy that occurs between us.

It has long been my intention to actively participate in creating my own spiritual, emotional, and physical health—recognizing that music is an essential part of that process. I became conscious of my desire to use music to create health in others about five years ago when my grandfather was dying. Although his body was tired and he was ready to die, his spirit still sought solace in things he found cathartic and familiar. He took keen pleasure in listening to his daughters and granddaughters sing old hymns at his bedside. And he loved the Stephane Grappelli tape I brought him, humming along with old standards like "Misty" and "Hold That Tiger."

It was at this same time that I was introduced to the concept of hospice care. I was amazed and thrilled to find that there was an organization devoted to helping with the life process of dying. I intuitively felt that organizations like hospice were ripe with opportunities to use music to create health and happiness.

As a preschool aide working for Idaho's early intervention program, I began consciously using music therapeutically in the classroom. Unlike patients receiving hospice care, the children I worked with were just beginning life. Their needs and capabilities ranged widely, but they all had a deep capacity to appreciate and participate in music. It was exciting to witness an autistic boy, who was usually withdrawn and unresponsive, dance and do the motions I taught him to "Singing in the Rain" and "Yankee Doodle." The lead teachers recognized my desire to develop and practice my own form of music therapy. They allowed me to direct music circles, create "transitional" music for children with particular behavioral struggles, and put together Christmas and spring programs performed by the children for parents and staff.

I have always recognized the power of music to create spiritual health in religious settings. As children, my three sisters and I accompanied my parents as traveling evangelists, singing and playing for mostly protestant congregations. The endless Family Von Trapp and Jackson Five (my maiden name is Jackson) jokes notwithstanding, these experiences were invaluable. I gained skills as a musician and performer and witnessed what one of my sisters calls the "tear factor"—the power my voice had to evoke emotional responses from my audience. These skills and lessons were integral to my adult desire to use music as a means of creating spiritual, as well as emotional and physical health.

Creating health and well-being in others through the use of music has contributed to my own musical development. Four years ago, I began teaching myself to play the guitar and to compose my own songs. The first song I wrote, a tribute to my elder sister, took several months to finish. The process, however challenging, was immensely rewarding and, after that first song, became easier and more natural.

I began creating "ceremonial" songs for the births of my nephews, weddings, and a love song for my sixth wedding anniversary. More recently I have been writing songs collaboratively with friends and family members. The give and take of collaborating with others is a wonderful opportunity to learn. It continues to teach me how to not let my ego subvert the creative process.

When I am centered and staying true to myself, I view the world through reverent eyes. I am able to see that everything I do has purpose and is sacred. Jon and I never planned our daily ritual of bonding through music. The process has always been so natural—maybe even primal—that it is easy to take for granted. I once heard an Aboriginal woman from Australia say that all of the members of her community were born artists and musicians. I believe this is true for all people, yet culturally it has often been easier to compartmentalize our abilities, creating arbitrary power struggles. It is my goal to ignore these barriers and recognize the musician (and artist, and athlete) in myself and in everyone I encounter. I would like to learn the skills of a music therapist in order to continue to facilitate my own, and other's healing through music.

*Liska McNally is the owner of Meadowlark Music Therapy in Portland, Oregon. She supervises internship and practicum students and is an adjunct faculty member at Marylhurst University.*

## Why I Want to Be a Music Therapist
## Letha L. Winger, MEd, SCMT, MT-BC

As I opened the filing cabinet door, a folder seemed to jump out at me. It was a folder I had never seen before labeled "Music Therapy." The searching exercise was part of an assignment. I needed to find a career about which I could be excited. Having at one time considered floral design, interpreting for the deaf, and psychology, I had yet to find it.

A sophomore at Brigham Young University, I had settled upon piano pedagogy, because I had played the piano since the age of eight, and I knew that I loved music. This was a career I could operate from home so that I could have and raise children.

The music department at Brigham Young was huge. The competition was excruciating, and I did not thrive in it. My talents did not tend toward technical accuracy, and it seemed I could not practice enough to get my music to sound as it was expected to sound. It was a constant struggle, and when I pondered about whether or not I would be able to find any joy in having students come to my home for piano lessons every day, I decided I was headed in the wrong direction.

I took the folder out and started to read. Immediately, I became excited. Here was a blend of psychology and music, which seemed a perfect fit for me. As I researched further, a feeling came over me that I cannot describe except to say that I knew that was where I belonged.

The next year, I transferred to Utah State University and began a year's worth of music therapy study with Dr. David Wolfe. During the following year, I married and moved back to Oregon. Though I was enthusiastically engaged in my education, it was then the right thing for me to do.

After marriage and moving back to Oregon, I worked in an office to help pay the bills while my husband figured out what he wanted his life's work to be. We then started a family. After my first son was born, in order to help with the bills, I decided to take some piano students. I have enjoyed teaching piano for the past thirteen years, and it indeed has been a wonderful way to be able to be home with my children. I am grateful for the many things I have learned in the process. I have enjoyed the relationships I have formed with the kids that come to my home each week. It is a joy to watch them succeed. However, the thing I have enjoyed most about teaching piano has little to do with tone quality or technical accuracy. It has little to do with expert playing or flawless finger work. What I love most about teaching is the way it helps students express their feelings. I love having them feel better when they walk out of my home. I love how they conquer some passage that is difficult. I love to help them play something that they didn't think they would be able to play. It is a joy to me to watch their successes resonate in their faces, their eyes, their smiles. To know that they feel better about themselves when they leave my home is the best feeling in the world.

This is why I want to be a music therapist. I want to be a facilitator of success. I want to be a coach for accomplishment. I want to be a builder of self-esteem. I want to be a bringer of laughter, fun, and joy. And, all the better, I'd like to do it with music.

I attended a lecture while at a music workshop at Brigham Young University in the early 1990s. It was given by Professor Rosalie Pratt. How I loved listening to her! She spoke about relaxation and how music was helping her ADHD grandson. She spoke about music and biofeedback and the latest research findings. We did an actual relaxation exercise in the auditorium while listening to Barber's "Adagio for Strings." It was fascinating! In fact, I attended the lecture twice. My feelings were so powerful that I didn't quite know what to make of it. I only knew that I wished to be doing something with music and medicine. I went home and subscribed to the *International Journal of Arts Medicine* and loved reading the articles therein. But my life was too demanding with young children. It wasn't the right time.

A couple of years ago, I attended a local music workshop in Beaverton, Oregon. One of the classes offered was a class that overviewed the field of music therapy. I cannot remember the name of the woman who presented that day, but she had also studied at Utah State University. She did a superb job, and I found myself a little depressed on my drive home.

But, still, the time was not right.

As I lay on my bed about six months ago, I was switching channels on the television, when I came across a woman giving a class about music therapy to a room full of adults. It was a cable access channel... local, I think. I don't remember the name or even the face of the woman doing the class, but as I watched what she was doing, tears streamed down my face, and I thought, *That's where I belong.*

But, the time still wasn't right.

The church I attend has a couple members who have handicapped children. I have had the opportunity to spend a little time with these children. It is a choice experience. One week, I was filling in for the youth music leader and happened to bring a few little instruments I have. It is, of course, a great novelty, and the children are very excited to play them while they sing. But oh what an experience it was when little Anthony, who is autistic, started playing his instrument. That made my day.

This past summer, I was visiting a friend in Washington. We embarked on a discussion about how we wanted to have a career at some point. We talked about how we would need to contribute to the income in our families in order to accommodate growing needs of our children in the future. We talked about going back to school. I remembered about being able to finish my degree from Brigham Young University with online courses, allowing me to receive a bachelor of general studies degree. It would be relatively inexpensive, and I could do it as I had the time. But then I pondered my career choices and realized that though it would be a little more difficult, financially and otherwise, the thing I wanted to do—have always wanted to do—is be a music therapist. As I have moved forward with plans to attend Marylhurst University, the road seems to clear ahead of me, and obstacles are moved with each step I take.

It is the right time. I am forty years old. I will admit to fear at reentering the scholastic world. But so far, the fear borders excitement with such similarity that sometimes I'm not sure which I am feeling. Having embarked on this endeavor, with each step, I am more sure of my course. I look forward to enriching the lives of others. I hope that I will be able to develop the skills with which to do this. I am thankful that there are those, so close by, who can assist me with this desire. Thank you.

*Letha L. Winger currently works as a hospice music therapist in Cache Valley, Utah. She is the clinical training director and instructor in the music therapy program at Utah State University.*

# Chapter 2: Finding a Music Therapy Program

At present, there are as many as seventy-four undergraduate programs in music therapy sprinkled among other liberal arts programs offered at colleges and universities throughout the country. This is a small number in comparison to about 160 occupational therapy programs and more than 265 speech and language pathology programs (allied health science sister professions) in the United States. Both were recognized as professions long before music therapy's official acceptance as a profession in 1950.

While there are undergraduate degrees under construction at colleges and universities, more institutions of higher education are including a graduate course of study in music therapy. The culture seems to be screaming for advanced training from college graduates. For both the student and the institution, this is a win-win situation. Institutions reap the benefits of increased enrollment, and for the student, it speaks of doors opening wider still in the market place. A music therapy degree provides for a real career path.

Advanced degrees in a profession do not necessarily equate to the well-prepared professional, because nothing takes the place of experience in one's field. However, the way of the world speaks loud and clear. Musicians are intuitively inclined to listen to the radar of cultural-speak. Young people hear that preparing for a field of work may eventually entail pursuing a graduate degree after completing an undergraduate program.

Pursuing a graduate degree in music therapy allows the therapist to specialize in and focus on a preferred interest, a population, area of academic teaching, or research. At present, more than thirty-five colleges and universities offer master's degrees in music therapy. This gives applicants a variety of philosophical and theoretical platforms from which to choose and enables more depth and breadth in an area of focus.

I recently interviewed a fourteen-year-old musician who was investigating music therapy as a profession. Nothing like getting a jump start on her career!

## American Music Therapy Association

The American Music Therapy Association (AMTA) was established in 2000 following the merger of two organizations: the National Association of Music Therapy (NAMT), founded in 1950, and the American Association of Music Therapy (AAMT), founded in 1971.

The AMTA holds an annual conference each fall, usually in November. As many as three hundred concurrent sessions are held in combination with a selection of institutes and specialized trainings prior to and following the conference. These conferences bring the news of current events and training about music therapy in the marketplace to the forefront for practitioners, and they are an energetic reminder of why we work as music therapists. Having attended and participated in many national conferences, I can attest to the renewal one feels when with colleagues from all over the world. It is an energizing experience to participate in a national conference of colleagues and friends. The conference also includes many exhibitors from the music industry, offering instruments at reduced rates, and booksellers promoting current and noteworthy music therapy resources.

## National Conferences

Seven regional conferences are held every spring throughout the country. These conferences offer a variety of concurrent sessions to attend depending on your interest and need for training. Conferences are also a wonderful opportunity for members to stay updated about music therapy's development on the national level.

Attending one or both of these conferences is vital to keeping your skills and cutting-edge practices alive. Being with colleagues from around the world also renews and inspires the spirit. See www.musictherapy.org for a list of the countries that belong to the AMTA.

# Chapter 3: Admission to a Music Therapy Program

The admission process for the prospective music therapy student varies among universities. In music departments that are oriented toward performance or that house a conservatory (University of the Pacific, Southern Methodist University, Shenandoah University, and others), a higher degree of musical expertise on a primary instrument is required. This may be a challenge for the student who has a well-rounded background on a variety of instruments. However, all music therapy programs assess the student's abilities on guitar, piano, and voice. Competency with these three instruments is required regardless of your competence on another instrument.

Filled with the dreams of all that the profession stands for, the music therapy student encounters the rigorous realities of achieving professional competency in more than 140 skills. Music therapy faculty and supervisors, skilled clinicians in their own right, passionately desire to help the music therapy student become successful. As Alex Fermanis states, "I learned the merit of practice and repetition toward a future goal. The skills such as persistence and perseverance that I have learned through making music have helped me in other areas of life and study."

## Program Requirements: Guitar, Piano, and Voice

All music therapy programs require an assessment of ability on guitar, piano, and voice, so every potential student should develop some musical strength on these instruments. Even if you've been playing the fiddle, ukulele, flute, horn, or drums for many years, you must be able to show some competence in these areas.

In addition to the musical requirements, a written essay on why you want to become a music therapist and a personal interview are required.

During the interview, the program director or designated faculty will assess your readiness in terms of attitude and motivation.

In the essays in this book, you can detect the common thread: the student's desire to help others and improve their lives through music's inherent ability to heal. The essays include the following statements:

- Jessica Western: "I have used music as an outlet for fear, joy, pain, and love. I am so excited there is an entire profession completely devoted to using music as a medium to communicate healing. I have been healed through music. I believe in it…I can think of no greater reward than using the musical talent God blessed me with to help people."

- Keeley Swete St. Clair: "My aspiration is that I can be one who brings music into others' lives and help them feel what music makes me feel: a deep peace and communion with self and community."

- Ted Owen: "I am drawn to pursue a career in music therapy primarily because I believe I can make a positive difference in the quality of life for others through my love and knowledge of the extraordinary connecting power of music."

- Alex Fermanis: "Using music to benefit others in any way, shape, or form is how I would like to function in the professional world."

- Alexis Bron: "Combining two areas I have a passion for, music and helping others, it seems to be the perfect career choice for me."

- Kara Ryan: "Music therapy will enable me to give voice to the trials and tribulations of others."

- Carla Carnegie: "Working with needs of others and spreading the healing powers that music has to offer."

- Jake Beck: "There exists in music an emotional relationship with all people, and I think in that relationship is the power to heal and to understand how to heal."
- Jennifer Ungarwulff: "All my life I have been drawn to help others. I seem to have a surplus of love and compassion."
- Liska McNally: "It is my goal to ignore these barriers and recognize the musician (and artist, and athlete) in myself and in everyone I encounter. I would like to learn the skills of a music therapist in order to continue to facilitate my own and other's healing through music."
- Melissa Potts: "I am looking forward to helping others through the gift of music."
- Karla O'Hagen Hawley: "I have come to deeply appreciate music as not only a teaching but also a healing application for a wide variety of people...I am dedicated to the belief in music and its application to heal, teach, and entertain."
- Megan Wilson Elliot: "I had been able to help someone, even if it was in the smallest way, feel a little better, and it made me feel so blessed. And that is when I knew I wanted to do that more. I wanted to do it every day if I could. I loved helping people feel better, cheering them up, giving them a reason to be hopeful and happy even while they are sick, alone, or afraid. Plus, there is a way to combine that with music, something else that I love and am passionate about! I just knew that it was what I wanted to do."

Like many of my faculty colleagues, over the years I have heard "using music to help others" consistently mentioned as a reason for wanting to become a music therapist. Although it may sound like a general anthem, when digging deeper, I find that the prospective student often expresses an almost vocation-like calling, a genuine desire to make things better for those less fortunate, and an authentic desire to be a peacemaker in a world filled with hurt.

Prospective students should check out the specific admission requirements and assessment process for the programs that interest them. In some music therapy programs, formal admission and audition on the three required instruments does not occur until the end of the freshman or sophomore year. The student will most often be asked to write an essay on why he or she wants to be a music therapist. This is followed by performing a song or two accompanied by either piano or guitar.

In most programs, students must demonstrate in a "jury" each semester sufficient progress in private vocal or instrumental instruction on their primary instrument. The jury is a private performance where members of the faculty preside along with the student's instructor. Strengths and weaknesses are noted on jury sheets so that the private instructor can discuss them with the student. This helps to keep the students advised at all times of their musical progress.

In the next chapter, I present some of the places in which music therapists find employment. This is not meant to be an exhaustive list, as new and varied employment sites are regularly added on the music therapy list serve. (The list serve is facilitated by a colleague from one of our music therapy programs.)

# Essays

## A Passion for People and Music
## Alexis Bron, MT-BC

According to Katherine Lindberg, MT-BC, music therapy can be defined as "the prescribed use of music and musical interventions in order to restore, maintain, and improve emotional, physical, physiological, and spiritual health and well-being." Music therapy is a highly respectable career that requires skilled individuals to combine music, teaching, and therapy in order to treat individuals with disorders or disabilities. The Berklee College of Music website on music therapy informs us that "a career in music therapy offers challenge, opportunity, and distinctive rewards to those interested in working with people of all ages with various disabilities." Music therapists can be found employed in numerous different settings/facilities. They work with many different types of people using music as the primary therapeutic tool. With this in mind, I have chosen to pursue music therapy as a career because of the versatility in which it can be used and the wide variety of people it involves, as well as its musical aspect.

In my research, I found that because music therapy is used in a number of different settings and facilities, it is a career with abundant opportunities. General hospitals, schools, correctional facilities, nursing homes, and a host of other care/treatment centers are some places where music therapists find jobs. Private practice is another option for music therapists as well as teaching classes at a university to train others to become music therapists. In a brief on music therapy, Kenneth Bruscia writes that "often, music therapists create their own positions by introducing themselves to administrators, demonstrating to the clinical staff what music therapy can do, and then consulting with the agency until a program can be initiated." In the past fifteen years especially, there has been an increase in the importance and need for trained music therapists due in part to the "increased awareness of the rights of children and adults with disabilities" (Foster). Because the value of music therapy is receiving steadily increasing recognition, employment opportunities are subsequently increasing (Berklee). Music therapy, unlike many other professions, offers numerous different options, which is one reason I am attracted to this career.

Music therapists are able to work with a wide variety of people. Some examples include the elderly, the mentally ill, individuals with learning disabilities, the physically handicapped, veterans, persons who have been abused, and the terminally ill. Kenneth Bruscia writes, "Because music therapists work with diverse populations, there are always opportunities to create new job openings." However, not just anyone can become a music therapist; there are certain qualities necessary to be competent in this profession. In order to effectively perform their job, music therapists must have musical playing ability as well as a genuine love for music. A background in music is also a plus. Some essential attributes music therapists need to possess are good physical and mental health, motivation, stamina, a maturity to work with exceptional individuals, self-awareness, and emotional stability. Other important qualities music therapists should have include patience, empathy, insight, and creativity. Probably most important though is that music therapists be caring and sensitive with a genuine interest in people and desire to help others. It is a logical choice to pursue a career in which I already possess many of the necessary qualities. I presently meet many of the above requirements; any I do not, I am willing to work to attain them.

Today, music therapy is an important and powerful tool in the lives of people to improve physical and mental health. As Senator Harry Reid said, "Simply put, music can heal people" (American Music Therapy Association). We do not know what the future holds for the direction of music therapy, but it will hopefully continue to expand, and its benefits will become more abundant and recognized. I want to be a part of this growing profession. I want to make an impact on the world beginning by making a difference in the peoples' lives in my career.

Music therapy is a career I will enjoy. Nothing seems more satisfying than using the powerful ability of music to connect with the body, soul, mind, and heart in a way that brings hope, healing, and restoration to individuals. Combining two areas I have a passion for, music and helping others, it seems to be the perfect career choice for me.

PS: 9/2014. I've been board certified for just over a year, and I've been working part time for the music therapy agency, Earthtones Music Therapy Services, with whom I interned. I am also teaching guitar lessons a few hours a week, working part time as a nanny/caregiver to three children, and running an online shop through Etsy where I sell my handmade craft items.

## References

American Music Therapy Association, http://www.musictherapy.org/about/quotes.

Berklee: Careers in Music Therapy, http://www.berklee.edu/careers/therapy.html.

Bruscia, Kenneth. Music Therapy Brief. Barcelona, 1993. Temple University: Boyer College of Music and Dance, http://www.temple.edu/musictherapy/home/program/faq.htm.

Foster, Ken. Foster Music Enterprises. 10 Dec. 2008. http://www.kenfoster.com/articles/careers.htm.

Lindberg, Katherine, http://members.aol.com/kathysl/def.html and http://members.aol.com/kathysl/questions.html.

*Alexis Bron works as a subcontractor for Earthtones Music Therapy Services in Portland, Oregon.*

## Why I Want to Be a Music Therapist
## Carla Carnegie, MT-BC

All of my life has been centered on music in some form: from the time I was a baby I heard folk songs and traditional music of Scandinavia, the British Isles, and America. My family says that from the time I was about two and able to crawl up on the piano bench, I would sit and plink out notes, finding some sort of tune or rhythm rather than just pounding keys to hear sound.

I begged for piano lessons, which I began at age seven. I loved learning to play the piano. My custom was to come home from school and sit at the piano and play for my own release and enjoyment, then settle into my lesson material. Mom always said she could tell the type of day I had had by what and how I would play. I didn't know the term "music therapy" at the time, but what I was doing was therapy for me. When I was happy, I played certain styles, and when I was sad, I played altogether different ones, and the way I approached my music was different depending on the mood. Music is such an important element in my life that I have often thought that if I had to lose one of my senses, I hope I don't lose hearing. Whatever would I do without being able to listen to music? I can play without seeing notes, but I can't fully enjoy music without hearing it!

By the time I was ten, I wanted to branch out into band instruments, but my dad would have none of it. In our house, we had all types of stringed instruments such as violin, mandolin, guitar, and banjo. If I wanted to take up another instrument, it would be one of those mentioned. I loved trying any instrument I could get my hands on, so I was disappointed in not getting to play a band instrument but not so much that I was unwilling to learn to play the violin. Along the way, I learned a handful of guitar chords as well, and while guitar is not my favorite instrument to play, I can get along with it.

Playing old-time music took me to nursing homes and retirement facilities where I saw the effect of the music that brought back memories for the older ones we played for. I remember staff telling me that one old gentleman was virtually unresponsive, until that is I played tunes of his time, and his toes began to tap, and the hands began to tap, and the eyes which before had been unimaginative began to twinkle. It was as if he "woke up." I remember enjoying the feeling that gave me. I made a difference in his life that day, and I wanted to repeat it again and again.

Over the years, I have played constantly either in an ensemble or solo the fiddle, accordion, piano, and percussive instruments. Teaching piano lessons and later fiddle lessons has been a source of joy and income. I always knew I wanted to go back to college and finish a degree, but I was indecisive as to what to focus on. As I raised my four children, I learned so much more about what I really wanted to do "when I grew up." It finally sunk into my being that it was music all along I wanted to get my degree in. The real question became, then what? What do I really want to do with that degree? I kept my eyes and my heart open, and a few things in written form crossed my path that told of how music could be used as therapy. That was my "aha" moment, and from then on, it was just plugging away on the degree while I got affirmation after affirmation that what I was being drawn to was what I feel God has been calling me to all my life. I am scheduled to earn my BA in music with an emphasis on composition this May 2009.

Along my life's journey, I have entertained older ones and young ones, taught lessons as I already mentioned, been a daycare provider and a caregiver for elderly parents, worked as a nurses aid in a nursing home and an assisted living facility where my mother resided before we had her live with us, been a temporary activity director at the same assisted living facility, been a travel agent, and been a tour guide for elders that were high-need travelers. I have also been active in church worship, helped with music for vacation Bible school, and am currently a substitute pianist/organist and choir director. Since the spring of 2007, I have had the honor of working in a women's drop-in shelter for homeless and low-income women. There, I have had experience with the mentally ill and seen the effect of music on them. It is an incredible thing how healing just listening to music being played can be. Over and over, I hear the comment, "When you play the piano, it calms me." Another employee and I offer women there free piano lessons. The women who come to the center teach me as much or more than I feel I do for them, which further inspires me to continue on this quest of using music in positive ways to enrich and help others. I truly feel that all of these activities and jobs have been preparing me for what I hope to be in a couple of years—a music therapist—working with needs of others and spreading the healing powers that music has to offer. What a fantastic way to spend the mature years of my life!

PS: After completing the academic requirements of the music therapy program, I went on to finish an extensive internship through Earthtones Music Therapy in Portland. I own and operate my private practice, Willow Song Music Therapy, where I serve individuals and groups living with developmental disabilities, autism, Parkinson's disease, dementia/Alzheimer's, well elders, and more. At this point, I travel to my clients in the Spokane, Washington, and Coeur d'Alene and Post Falls, Idaho, areas, providing treatment in their private home, assisted living facility, retirement facility, adult family home, resource center, and public community center. I also conduct workshops on stress management/wellness for the public, using music recreationally to benefit individual well-being. In the near future, Willow Song will be expanding to incorporate a music therapy space shared with other therapies to bring more access to individuals needing music therapy. Teaching music lessons on piano and violin for typically functioning individuals, and adaptive lessons for individuals needing a unique approach, rounds out my practice. Additionally, consulting, music notation/transcription services, playing in a band, and serving as a church pianist hones other skills as a musician. Being a business owner requires and utilizes a whole other skill set of which I am on a continual learning curve. Being a music therapist in an area where there is little knowledge of or use of music therapy motivates me to continually put myself out there to conduct presentations, in services, etc., endeavoring to further educate the public and advocate for this profession that I am so honored to be a part of.

## Music Therapy Entrance Essay
## Alex Fermanis, MT- BC

"Music, a form of human behavior, is unique and powerful in its influence."—Thayer E. Gaston

During the past eight years of music making, I have reveled in the influence that music has had on me and the people around me. I have seen the positive influence of music manifest itself in others in many forms and incarnations. When utilized properly, music becomes a powerful solution for daily and lifelong problems. This form of creation and expression, having such a powerful influence, is a field in which there is much to contribute and contrive.

Music has served as a constant while everything around me has changed. Whether playing in an orchestra or jamming with friends, music has always been a perpetuation of joy and expression. I remember getting up at dawn every Saturday for five years to catch the early ferry to Seattle in order to rehearse with the Seattle Youth Symphony. Barely awake and somewhat grumpy, my mood was transformed after three hours of rehearsing classical masterpieces. These three hours changed my grumpiness to radiating happiness and my incredible fatigue to a burning energy that carried me throughout my day. Having started out with an emphasis on formal and written music, I learned the merit of practice and repetition toward a future goal. The skills such as persistence and perseverance that I have learned through making music have helped me in other areas of life and study. Living with two artists as parents further reinforced the importance of expression and creation. Even though our mediums of expression aren't the same, they still convey an attempt at expressing life and all it encompasses.

Aaron Copland said, "So long as the human spirit thrives on this planet, music in some living form will accompany and sustain it and give it expressive meaning." I feel that this quotation best sums up my own thoughts and ideas toward the importance of music in everyday life. For a musician, it is a constant expression of life and living; for a listener, it is an ever-changing representation of ideas, concepts, and opinions. Music has a way of reaching out to most people in a way that is both profound and beautiful. When one thinks about it, every momentous occasion in one's life can be punctuated with music appropriate to that occasion: for example, a graduation, wedding, or funeral. People select the music that touches their hearts in a most personal way. This is exactly why I would like to employ music as a therapeutic tool, because it tends to have such a wide reach and profound effect. Music is a representation/expression of the human condition.

Now that I have completed three years of music study, I am ready to delve into the more scientific and observant aspect of music in therapeutic form. Through the understanding of the motives and drives of the human mind, I have seen more and more opportunities where music therapy can be applied. I have personally seen music's effect on several children while baby-sitting. When music is either played live or played as an interactive activity with the children, they become focused and enthralled. I believe that the sound they create, even if cacophonous, gives them a sense of empowerment and a basic harness to their creativity. These personal realizations and revelations have pushed me all the more toward a focus on using music in conjunction with therapy. Another redeeming quality of music is that regardless of language, culture, or location, one can still communicate in some way through the act of creation.

In a rapidly changing world, living in a fast-paced, profit-based society can do a lot to a person stress wise. I believe there is a need to investigate more reasonable solutions to alleviate stress through homeopathy and naturopathy. Using music instead of prescription drugs in certain cases to cure an ailment such as lack of focus or depression would seem to be all the more preferable. Even the simple act of putting on a Brahms symphony or a Chopin prelude can do much to stimulate the mind and relax the body.

The personal impact that music has made in my life and in that of my close friends and family is so great that it must be shared not only on a community level but also in the medical and therapeutic community worldwide. Music has brought with it constant happiness since my discovery of it eight years past. I feel that it is therefore my duty to continue to spread the gift and benefits of music making and appreciation as I continue with my studies. Using music to benefit others in any way, shape, or form is how I would like to function in the professional world. The future of therapeutic care must encompass the arts and the many stimuli they possess to effectively aid the human mind and body.

Works Cited: Gaston, E. Thayer, *Music in Therapy*. New York: Macmillan, 1968.

*Alex Fermanis is now assisting Karla O'Hagen Hawley in her work with the Music Project in Everett, Washington.*

## Music Therapy Essay
## Karla O'Hagen Hawley, MEd, MT-BC

At a young age, I was given many challenges and opportunities to realize not one but two passions: teaching children and the playing and enjoyment of piano. These two passions existed simultaneously, though separate, until many years ago. The director of my son's preschool asked me to provide a multifaceted arts program for the school. As a volunteer, it was in this setting that my two passions became entwined.

In 1994, I began teaching children basic music theory and combined it with math, science, art and movement, hands-on exploration, and personal experience that translated into their play. The primary objective was to stimulate and enhance the young minds of children through music. The curriculum evolved and produced the question "how does music affect a child's ability to learn?" This question culminated in my master's in education thesis work, "Music Integrated Vocabulary Development in First Grade Students." Next question, "Where will I be able to apply this new knowledge?"

This year, music therapy appeared at a magical moment. My son will be graduating from high school in 2008, and my husband has offered unconditional support for my return to school in an effort to further explore the 1994 music curriculum. From the one and only music therapy class taken to date, I have come to deeply appreciate music as not only a teaching but also healing application on a wide population of people. More than twenty-three hundred years ago, Plato said, "Music is a more potent instrument than any other for education and children should be taught music before anything else." I cannot imagine spending my life's energies in any other arena. I am dedicated to the belief in music and its application to heal, teach and entertain.

PS: What am I doing now? Where have my two passions led me?

I am The Good Pirate of the Northwest, sort of like The Good Witch of the North in the story *The Wizard of Oz*. I could easily break into song about sailing the high music seas on a ship made only of instruments, a ship that would never sink and that holds the hearts and souls of individuals that climb aboard looking for peace and solution to their ills. I would write about pleasingly plundering all populations, but, alas, that would only satisfy my humor and perhaps others. The metaphor of a pirate appeals to me because the journey has been rough and rewarding. Rough because I never had to work so hard at school to understand music theory, endure juries, practicums, annual/quarterly/tri-mesterly musical skill assessments on piano, voice, and guitar, and rough because of the simultaneous personal transformation that occurred. I could have completed the program in two years because of my previous educations (BS in psych/biology and master's in education), but instead I chose the four-year path, knowing my passions would require support from an inner strength and wisdom that would only come from taking the time to know at every moment where I was on the ever-changing healing musical map (another pirate metaphor—argh!).

The becoming of a music therapist has required a brave and adventurous heart: I must know my inner seas, oceans, and waterways like the back of my hand in order to navigate the myriad of music therapy sessions with traumatized populations who in turn require help navigating their way toward a safe harbor of health. The rewards, I am thrilled to say, are endless: sustainability in self, friends, colleagues, and the wisdom to accept the knowledge of what I can change and what I cannot not, that there is a greater purpose for me that I cannot see but know in my heart-map that I am on the right course. Wherever it may take me!

*Karla O'Hagen Hawley, MEd, MT-BC, is the music therapist for the Snohomish County Music Project in Washington and the owner of RAP IT Music Therapy Services, LLC.*

## Why I Wish to Become a Music Therapist
## Ted Owen, MT-BC

In early spring of 2003, I read *The Healing Power of the Drum* by Robert Lawrence Friedman. Upon reading the first fifty to sixty pages or so, I found myself moved to the point of welling up several times. Needless to say, this got my attention in a big way and sparked an interest, more of a personal mission actually, that has brought me along the path to becoming a music therapist. Within the text of Friedman's book are numerous individual anecdotes from practicing music therapists as well as other healthcare professionals and musicians giving testimony to the power of music as a means for achieving positive therapeutic results within a wide range of populations (clinical and otherwise). These stories are simply amazing and inspiring. And I have become hooked.

My continuing personal relationship with music began as a young boy taking piano lessons and spans the forty-six years that have followed. As a budding percussionist, I was mindful early on of the value of playing music just for the joy of it. Coming home from school as a teenager and being able to sit behind a set of drums and purge many pent-up frustrations of adolescence was a natural way for me to take care of myself. A performing musician for the better part of twenty years, I have also experienced firsthand, and in profound depth, what it means to share in the making of music with others. As I continue to discover and learn more and more about music therapy and its many health-benefiting applications, the notion of sharing this joy so that others may heal is very compelling to me. This is something much more meaningful to this musician than simply performing before an audience. It is my passion.

During the time since reading Friedman's book, I have sought and received wonderful guidance and training from many dedicated individuals within the music therapy profession. After taking the Introduction to Music Therapy course offered at Marylhurst University this past fall, I became even more aware of the collective value that the profession brings to society as a whole and the many opportunities available for me to become actively involved and make a very real contribution.

I am drawn to pursue a career in music therapy primarily because I believe I can make a positive difference in the quality of life for others through my love and knowledge of the extraordinary connecting power of music. I wholeheartedly look forward to attending Marylhurst University to earn the credentials qualifying me to become a certified music therapist.

*Ted Owen works as an independent contractor with Earthtones Music Therapy Services in Portland, Oregon.*

## Audition Essay
## Melissa Potts, MEd, MT-BC

About fifteen years ago, while attending Southwestern Community College in Southern California, 1 found myself staring at a dot matrix computer printout on careers I may be suited for. Among piano teacher, general music teacher, and performer was a heading titled "Music Therapist." At the time, I thought, "What is this?" I had never heard of this occupation before, and no one else at the career center had either. Somehow I even felt self-conscious about learning more about it, as if this was some type of taboo field meant for people who couldn't make it in the music profession. (I had very low self-esteem at the time and was struggling with the notion of what I was meant to be when I grew up.) I just printed out whatever I could find on the topic only to read about it and kind of filed it away in my mind.

After a few years at Southwestern, I decided to pick a career so I could hang something on the wall to account for all the credits I had racked up. I decided to transfer to San Diego State University as a music education major. I wasn't exactly sure what that degree would do for me. I just felt that somehow I would find out what I was meant to do in life.

Let me digress for a moment to tell you that while I was at Southwestern, I took every class that ever held an inkling of interest to me. I took ceramics and found out 1 was absolutely horrible at it. I took art history, which was kind of fun but hard. Other classes included small business management (I was great at this!), jazz combo, musical theatre, chamber singers, choir, saxophone and piano lessons, aerobics, and many more. I even took an EMT training class thinking I might save people in an emergency. 1 always went back to music. For me, it was easier to find out what I didn't want to do than what I did want to do.

Through the four years at SDSU, I held several waitressing and cocktailing jobs and played piano for children's theater and many different theater groups around town. I also was in a top forty wedding and corporate/casual band, playing keyboards and singing. After I graduated, I found that I could not complete the credential program and pay my rent at the same time. (The program required that you not hold a job.) I put my credential on hold and decided to take a break from school.

In 1996, I decided to inquire about that job title I'd read about ten years earlier. I found an Introduction to Music Therapy class offered at Chapman College at a San Diego branch. I went for it! I loved this class and all the things we learned. I felt enlightened. I was finally free of doubt. I even called an old college professor over Christmas break and happily proclaimed on her voice mail that I finally had found my calling. I was meant to be a music therapist!!!

Everything about the field seemed exciting and interesting. The idea of using music almost as a medicine to improve the lives of autistic children, Alzheimer's patients, and developmentally disabled people was so intriguing.

As I neared completion of the class, other students were making plans to carpool and do the ninety-minute drive to the Orange County campus to take part two of the class. I was faced with some personal challenges and got sidetracked. My uncle, grandmother, and father passed away suddenly within six weeks of each other. My mom and family were devastated. I was in shock. I flew back and forth from San Diego to Oregon a few times to be with my mom and help her with things. Now that I reflect back, I can see how music even played a major part in comforting my mom through that period. My dad had been involved with opera and musical theatre for years, and my mom carefully picked out the music and taped everything for his service. We looked at pictures, listened to his old recordings, and celebrated his life through music.

After that, life happened. I joined two different bands, got married, had two kids, and got divorced (all within nine years), and now I'm starting over. I feel that the time is right in my life to pursue music therapy. I've read so much about it, I feel that I have a contribution to make and that I would he great at it. I'm not sure exactly which population I would like to work with the most; however, I do love kids and young people.

This last school year, I had the opportunity to work for the Salem-Keizer School District as a part-time general music teacher (elementary school level.) My favorite time of day was when my DLC students arrived. We would play games with music, and I quickly learned what kind of music got them revved up and what would calm them down. I learned from them as they learned from me. The group consisted of eleven students, all with different abilities. I was told I was there as almost an entertainer rather than a music teacher. This didn't sit very well with me, because I felt I had more of a duty to have a goal and work toward it. This was a challenge, but we did master some basic skills together.

I have high hopes of attending the music therapy program at Marylhurst University; I am looking forward to helping others through the gift of music.

*Melissa Potts works in the inpatient psychiatric unit at Salem General Hospital in addition to offering private music therapy services in Salem, Oregon.*

## Music Therapy Essay
## Kara Ryan, MT-BC

My enthusiasm for the field of music therapy has grown and been reaffirmed as I continue to discover more about this unique profession. As my familiarity with this fascinating career develops, so does my clarity about my personal aspirations and professional goals. I've found that my goals for personal and professional growth naturally converge with the career path of the music therapist.

I was first introduced to music therapy at the time that I was initially applying to colleges. While music therapy sparked my interest, I had numerous other subjects of interest like English, art, psychology, women's issues, and health and wellness. I wanted to explore these interests, and I was not yet ready to commit to attending a school specifically for the music therapy major. At that point in time, I knew as little about music therapy as I did about what I wanted to study in school. During my freshman year of college, I was informally on a vocal performance track while also taking a few classes in my other interests. I spent much of my freshman year trying to figure out what role I wanted music to play in my life and where it fit with my other interests. I came to realize that I was not interested in pursuing the competitive career of music performance but rather that music was something I did, in large part, for my own personal wellness. Music was and remains my tool for self-discovery and is a necessary component for maintaining balance in my life. However, I have also come to recognize that I would not be content to make music merely as a hobby, and I do not want to remove it entirely from my academic studies. I know that in choosing a non-music course of study or career, music would get pushed aside, and I would not have the time or resources to pursue some of my lifelong musical goals. (One such goal is gaining competency in guitar and piano so that I might put some of my writing to music, etc.)

With this recent self-discovery, I have been determined to find a more focused course of study, school, and/or degree program that will allow me to integrate music and my interests in psychology, social work, and art. The options are few, but I am brought back to what I now recognize to be a uniquely perfect program for me: music therapy. The more research that I do on the field, the more confident I am that this is the career for me.

In addition to providing the opportunity to further my musicianship, the music therapy degree offers me the chance to address my concerns of health and wellness, especially in the emotional and spiritual realms. I've long been interested in alternative approaches to medicine and therapy, but I am overwhelmingly excited to find that music and art are becoming respected and accepted forms of complementary treatment. It must be exciting for any artist or musician to see that science is now supporting the belief in the healing power of the arts. Currently, there is a perceived shift in the philosophy of healthcare, a movement away from objective and impersonal care toward a more comprehensive care for the "whole person." This trend was recently confirmed in an interview I had with Dana Sheppard, a therapeutic musician and head of the complementary therapies program at Harrison Hospital, Silverdale/ Bremerton, Washington. She claims that these alternative therapies (music, art, pet visits, etc.) are the "humanizing elements" for enhancing the hospital experience. Ms. Sheppard also pointed out a beneficial bonus of using music therapeutically: the effect of music in a given environment is contagious. Musicians playing at the hospital assume that their playing is primarily for the patients and guests. However, the music has been observed to relieve stress in the hospital staff while also helping the patients. When the staff is more at ease, the work is performed with greater efficiency and in a friendlier manner toward both coworkers and patients. These two aspects of music therapy (being a humanizing element, and music therapy easing stress for staff and patients alike) reiterate my passion for music and its amazing power for helping people.

While it is my passion for music, wellness, and people that leads me to pursue a career in music therapy, the diverse opportunities and environments in which to practice music therapy are immensely appealing to me. I could be working with any variety of people from youth to geriatrics or those with physical, mental, or emotional conditions. I could also be working in a multitude of environments from hospitals to schools. Having this many choices would allow me to be constantly learning from new challenges and to change where and whom I work with as would best fit with the changes in my life. For example, currently I'm most interested in working with emotionally distraught youth, maybe even traveling and doing this cross-culturally. I can also see myself working with women who are working to overcome addictions, etc. in an environment like a halfway house. There is also the option of opening a private practice. This autonomy is important to me as is the inherent requirement/opportunity for creativity and improvisation. Perhaps most important to me is the idea that I will be growing as much as the people with whom I work and interact.

Albert Schweitzer once said, "Joy, sorrow, tears, lamentation, laughter—to all these music gives voice but in such a way that we are transported from the world of unrest to a world of peace and see reality in a new way." Music therapy will enable me to "give voice" to the trials and tribulations of others. I know that this will be a personal journey for me, and I am excited to share with others the comfort, healing, and hope that I have found in music.

*Kara Ryan was employed by Children's Hospital in Chicago. She is now pursuing her master's degree in creative arts therapy at Prescott College in Arizona.*

## A Call to Music Therapy
### Keeley Swete St. Clair, MT-BC

Music is much more than a choice for me. It is my calling. Music is one of those inherent drives in my body that pulls me toward it insatiably. As I have traveled through my life, music has been the defining dynamic. I can't remember a time growing up that I wasn't singing or playing music. Likewise, the personal need in me for empathy and compassion toward others has led me to this point. Life has positioned me perfectly, it seems to this very moment, with this great urge for using music to help my clients live their best lives. This is the story of my journey, about how I came to know that music therapy was my true calling.

Altruistic thoughts concerning music, however, haven't always been there for me. It started like anything else: a discovery, the strange familiarity, and the feeling that it is yours and yours alone, to be shared but never fully given. This was my experience with music for many years. I felt that my music was mine, that intense personal gratification and connection one feels when your voice merges with the music was an intensely personal experience. I felt powerful, calm, and exhilarated all at once; nothing else in my experience had ever made me feel so connected and at peace with myself. It wasn't until I graduated high school and was a year into college at the University of Oregon that the notion grasped me that music could make others feel what I felt, that I could help facilitate that feeling for them through my passion for music.

At eighteen years old, I enrolled in the music program at the University of Oregon with a major in vocal performance. I remember feeling so full of hope and anticipation. I attended an orientation session for the School of Music, during which one professor of music said that the majority of us would change our major during our time at the university. I can still remember the dash of thoughts that flew through my head at that time. I truly believed that I would *not* be included in that majority. I literally couldn't imagine doing anything else but music.

A year into the music program, my feelings began to change. I began taking classes in women's studies and environmental studies, feeling a strong connection to both. I began thinking about different possibilities for myself and wondering if a degree in music really was for me. A transformation began to occur within me. I began to feel a greater responsibility to bring a more positive impact to the world through my actions. I knew then that I had to devote my life to a meaningful type of work, a cause that would positively change the world we live in. I had begun to feel that music training at the University of Oregon was stifling to my musical creativity rather than an inspiration to it. Likewise, I just couldn't see how a degree in vocal performance could make a true and positive impact to the world around me. By the end of my second year at UO, I had changed my mind—to what, I still wasn't sure. Although I still had an immense passion for music, there were so many things that I hadn't experienced. New ideas were forming within me about the world and my place in it.

I decided to take some time off of school to live inside my new philosophy and find true meaning in my life aspirations. At about twenty, I began an intense spiritual journey and rediscovered a circle of friends I had made in high school who were on the same path as me. We were all striving to connect with spirit, to make a positive impact on this planet, to discover our truth and meaning. We began making music together. We wrote, jammed, recorded, and shared completely with each other our music. The feeling of unity was palpable and changed us forever. We began to invite others into our circle to share the experience. Everyone was hooked, and the newcomers were intoxicated with the sense of community and connection to music. As I watched these strangers' faces light up and smiles flash, my thoughts regarding music as a therapy tool began to solidify.

I knew there was a possibility that music could help people in a real and meaningful way. I began to research music as a type of therapy and soon learned that music therapy was an existing reality, an actual vocation. I finally had my "ah ha" moment. Everything shifted into place, and I was certain that this was meant for me.

Unfortunately, what's meant to be and what actually happens sometimes aren't in sync with each other. I was working as a restaurant manager at the time and really enjoying living life for life's sake. I wasn't ready to go back to school just yet. Truthfully, I couldn't bear the thought of going back through music school again; it had all been so overwhelming for me when I was younger.

One thing I knew for sure was I really wanted to offer my hand and heart to others. I also knew that a traditional career in therapy, although greatly rewarding, was not something I was interested in. Soon after, I tried my hand at massage therapy. I seemed like a good fit conceptually, yet I knew from the beginning that it wasn't my true calling. I listened to my colleagues talk about their pull toward the art of massage, and I tried to feel what they felt, but after a year, I knew that it wasn't the right fit. I kept pushing the thoughts of music therapy back, knowing that I'd have to return to music school and dreading it. It was around this time that I met my husband, who is also a musician. He inspired me to walk toward my true self and conquer my anxiety toward music school. I knew I couldn't be anything but true to myself for as long as we were together, so I decided to stop hiding from what I really wanted. We were married in the summer of 2005, and that same summer, I decided I would go back to school in the fall. I quit my management position at a fine dining restaurant so I could focus on my education and faced head on the anxieties I had about school

For the last three years, I have been working diligently on my music skills with therapy in mind at Lane Community College. A fusion of a developing maturity level, the passing of time, and resolve to succeed has helped me to excel in my studies at Lane. All my experiences thus far have drawn me to this insight that music therapy will realize the inherent drives within me. I have found that I am most enthusiastic about working with high-needs children. Although many client populations are a possibility, working with children who have physical, mental, and/or developmental challenges feels like the right fit for me. Fueled by curiosity and possibility, I have researched music therapy methods and have become even more inspired by the application itself.

I find it fascinating that one can help clients learn valuable life skills in a different way, a way that works with the client in mind. I believe that using music as a device toward a better-lived life, that the ability for clients to learn new practical life skills without even realizing that they are making leaps and bounds socially, is astounding. Something so simple as hand-eye coordination, sharing, or eye contact can make an immense difference in a high-needs client's life. All these things and much more are addressed using music therapy as the inspiring factor, and I am highly motivated to use these tools with my clients in order to give them the experience in life that they truly deserve. As a music therapy hopeful, I am moved to learn as much as I can and to employ the learned methods with the utmost professionalism, compassion, and integrity.

Thus, we come full circle. From the indecisive young woman eager to explore new possibilities to the determined and willing woman I am today, the thought of music therapy has fueled my appetite to succeed. As fate would have it, I stand before you almost a decade after having an epiphany about my life aspiration. Music therapy truly is the synthesis of my two passions. My intense love for music and determined drive to make a difference culminate perfectly. Just as determined and inspired as I was all those years ago toward music therapy, I will work hard to graduate and someday give my clients a feeling of accomplishment and great reward from music. I see the world today as unfortunate: bleak and begging for individuals to step forward and make a difference. Although it might not make an instant and immense change in the world, one by one people will take back their lives with the help of music, and in the long run, the impact will be relevant and vast. My aspiration is that I can be one who brings music into others' lives and help them feel what music makes me feel: a deep peace and communion with self and community. I have faith that the good I am able to do for my clients will ripple out exponentially, gradually causing greater and greater events to transpire, and that it will cause a grand and positive impact on this planet.

*Keeley Swete St. Clair works as a subcontractor for Earthtones Music Therapy Services in Portland, Oregon.*

## Why I Want to Be a Music Therapist
## Jennifer Ungarwulff, MT-BC

Eugene is home to a large, stately retirement residence by the name of Sheldon Park. Tucked away in its southeast corner is the Alzheimer's and dementia ward, Kingswood. The residents of Kingswood live in a foggy and incoherent world, a world filled with shadows of the lives they have lost the ability to live.

Janet is a Kingswood resident. She sits complacently in her chair, perpetually staring into the distorted confusion of her mind. She seldom responds when addressed. On those lucky occasions when her attention can be obtained, she responds negatively to most suggested activities.

I have been working with Janet and others like her for more than six months. During this time, I have gotten to know many of the residents suffering from Alzheimer's in addition to learning hands on about the many facets of this tragic and mystifying disease. As an employee in the activities department, it is my challenging job to involve these residents in activities that most of them are willing or able to do.

Recently I decided to compile several books of song, choosing selections known by the residents. My hope was to lead them in a sing-along. The results have been extremely encouraging. Seventeen out of the twenty residents joined in singing classics from "I've Been Working on the Railroad" to "Auld Lang Syne." I have not witnessed as much participation and positive response in any other activity, especially in Janet's case. Normally devoid of any expression, Janet comes roaring to life with an eager and spirited rendition of "Take Me Out to the Ball Game," finishing with a broad grin and chuckle.

Another striking example of the transformative power of music comes from Eva. Eva is a resident who wanders from the time she rises till the time she goes to sleep. She seldom speaks, but when she does, only incoherent mumblings can be heard. She is plagued by a confused agitation that seems to surround her every movement. On one special Sunday, Eva wandered in as I led the group in singing. Much to my amazement, she stopped, turned to me, and sang the last verse to "Amazing Grace." Afterward she said with a smile, "That was great." I was completely shocked. To one who does not know Eva, singing a few lines from a song might seem insignificant. However, to me, it was a moving and inspiring experience. Music, in Eva's case, seemed to restore some basic cognitive abilities. Working with music daily has kindled a strong desire to make music the permanent focus of my life, at the same time inspiring me to explore the therapeutic element of music.

My experiences at work support my belief in the beauty of music, in its power to awaken intense emotions in people, and its intrinsic capacity to calm and heal.

Music for me has always been therapeutic. When I am feeling stressed out or upset, sad, or depressed, I can turn on a favorite song or album, and inevitably my mood will improve. Music helps bring people closer together whether joining in appreciation of a recording or a live concert.

I have often noticed a strong connection when musicians come together. They can be perfectly in sync and possess an understanding that communicates a musical idea from the heart of one person to another, a communication of immeasurable depth that goes beyond what words can describe. As a universal language, music brings harmony, understanding, and unity in a world wrought by political and social unrest.

My love for music is my strongest passion. The sensation I experience when singing, either alone or accompanied, is unlike any other. An overwhelming feeling of serenity fills my body, giving me a sort of rapturous joy. My voice has been the one constant source of satisfaction and happiness in my life. When I sing for or with others, that happiness is amplified.

All my life I have been drawn to help others. I seem to have a surplus of love and compassion. Whether animal, plant, or human, I have always been strongly driven to help. I cannot imagine a better vocation than one that intertwines my altruistic and creative abilities. I want to work in an environment that allows me to introduce others to the beauty of music both inside and outside of themselves and to essentially teach healing through sound. I honestly can't think of an occupation more aptly suited to me. The idea of studying music therapy and of practicing it infuses me with excitement and a real sense of purpose. *Jennifer Ungarwulff, MS, NCC, MT-BC (Marylhurst University)*

## Why I Wish To Become a Music Therapist
### Jessica Western, MT-BC

I am the love child of two long-haired hippie musicians. When I was old enough to walk and talk, the question was not *if* I would play an instrument; the question was *what* instrument that would be. I chose the flute, and somewhere along the line came guitar, piano, voice, dance, painting, poetry…I simply cannot live without the arts, specifically music. It is my passion. That being said, I always knew I would pursue a career in the musical arena.

I was often principal flute in many ensembles, both in school and through competitions, so I logically considered performance first. After talking to other performance majors and professional flutists, I found that performance for me would be too limiting and self-oriented. I want to help people in a personal and firsthand way, so next I considered music education. Upon high school graduation, I was offered (and accepted) a woodwind instructor position at a local high school teaching students only one year younger than myself! I continued to teach at Marcos de Niza High for the past two years, but I knew something was still missing. I was good at teaching and enjoyed it immensely, but again I felt like it just wasn't the perfect fit for me.

My mother has lupus, and I first heard about music therapy last year when she had to be hospitalized. Her doctor suggested getting with the music therapist on site to help her relax and therefore possibly boost her immunity system. She benefited greatly from her sessions with the music therapist, and I started digging around and researching what I could. The more I found out (and continue to learn), the more I was both captivated and interested.

Everything about music therapy makes perfect sense to me and for me. Growing up, I would often lock myself in my bathroom for hours and just play music. Music is, to me, the most complete medium of communication. I have used music as an outlet for fear, joy, pain, and love. I am so excited there is an entire profession completely devoted to using music as a medium to communicate healing. I have been healed through music. I believe in it.

When my aunt was diagnosed with breast cancer, I packed my guitar and my flute and drove to Las Vegas to visit her. I sat by her bedside and sang her favorite hymns for an entire weekend. Her doctor noticed her lowered blood pressure, and everyone was surprised when she slept that weekend, painlessly and peacefully without the aid of medication.

I want to learn all I can. Not only do I desire to be a music therapist, I think I am a perfect candidate to be a great one. I play the flute, an instrument with a soothing and therapeutic timbre. I am not the most accomplished pianist or guitar player, but I can accompany myself singing just fine. I am comfortable with chording and improvisation within a given key. I have done plenty of volunteer work and am comfortable with special populations (children, elderly, autistic children, and burn victims). Lastly, I am comfortable in clinical environments.

I have been enjoying youth, independence, and a job I love but have also been dragging my feet at community college for two years. I wanted to be sure before I began to pursue a specific degree. I am not only sure now but also excited and ready to throw my whole self into achieving the first step: a bachelors in music therapy.

Why do I want to be a music therapist? Because I want a rewarding career I enjoy. And I can think of no greater reward than using the musical talent God blessed me with to help people.

*(Jessica recently added the following to her original essay.)*

PS: It is over eleven years since I wrote this entrance essay. The fact that Christine Korb has held onto it all these years and could share it now and include it in this publication is testament to the type of educator she is: one who truly mentors (from the heart and spirit, not just the mind), takes the long view (taking every opportunity to remind one how far they've come), and holds dear every student whose life she has touched, and also is apparently one who keeps extremely organized files! I completed my clinical education, was successfully board certified, and have been a music therapist for the past five years.

When I read this entrance essay, I hear the voice of myself past. I hear all the fervor and ambition, all the soul and openness, a little naiveté, and a lot of hope. But the clarity with which I heard and was trying to heed the calling I felt then is still there, perhaps now more than ever, as I find myself more professionally satisfied at this present moment than I have ever been before in my life. I am still heeding the call I felt to this profession. Every day only demonstrates further the extent to which this is my life's work, and I am endlessly fulfilled in doing it. In doing this work, I feel in alignment with my highest potentials as a musician, as a therapist, and as a human being.

The entrance essay describes how personal the embarkation into my education was. I provided music for my aunt with breast cancer and got to experience results firsthand before I even knew what I was truly doing. I learned about music therapy during a time when my mother was hospitalized and a music therapist knocked on her hospital room door.

Eleven years later, the next chapter in how my personal journey resulted in a clarifying of my professional goals is about my grandmother. Last year, I moved into my grandparents' home to assist my grandfather in caring for my grandmother, who left this world in October 2013. Her last wish was to die at home, and this required my whole family to rally around my grandfather. My grandmother was very dependent on him for caregiving in her decline (the cancer was metastasized throughout her body), and it was not a peaceful or easy process. But music provided a way to change the environment (away from stress and toward loving acceptance), to ease her pain (through soothing alternate engagement), to express her final messages (we wrote a song about her life, her legacy, and her process of physically letting go), and to ease the suffering of all of us as we watched our matriarch fade away and each attempted our goodbyes.

A year later, I am a music therapist with a local hospice agency, and I find that rather than just retrigger my own grief, providing music therapy to patients at the end of their life is a deeply honoring, fulfilling service that I know Nana would be so proud of me for providing. I consider my clinical hospice practice to be a part of her legacy. Her hospice journey is what broke ground on the deep well of compassion from which I draw daily in providing hospice care. I also supervise practicum students in the field and teach courses as an adjunct faculty member in the program I graduated from. This is something I recently began, so the quality I feel of returning home, coming full circle, etc. is definitely a defining aspect of my life right now. I look in the eyes of my freshman students, and I see them heeding the call that I was beginning to heed in this entrance essay. I am blessed to have had a great example of how to help them remain true to that calling and true to themselves and their own unique contribution to this amazing field. From the bottom of my heart, thank you, Chris.

*Jessica Western is a practicum supervisor and adjunct faculty member for Marylhurst University and a music therapist with Willamette Valley Hospice in Salem, Oregon.*

## Music Therapy Essay
## Megan Elliot Wilson, MT-BC

When I was a senior in high school, I was sure that I had my life all figured out. I would go to college, get my degree in music, go on to get my master's degree in teaching, and then become a high school or college choir director. However, my experience as music major turned out to be a lot different than I expected. My plan was to just do general music, but then I found how much I enjoyed my voice lessons and classes, and I also developed a huge love for opera. So I switched my major to vocal performance to give my major more depth and also because I was determined to improve as a singer. As difficult as it was, this proved to be very fruitful and beneficial for me, and giving my senior recital (as frightening as it may have been) is one of my most cherished memories.

Through all of this, however, I was struggling, because I remembered my grand plan to get my master's and become a teacher, but in my heart, I was not sure that I felt called to be a teacher. This caused a lot of hesitation on my part, because the last thing I wanted to do was become a teacher because I felt that it was the next logical step or that it was the only thing I could do career wise. I wanted to be passionate about it and have that be passed on to the students. So I decided not to apply for a master's program right away and to give myself some time to really think about what I wanted to do.

After I graduated in May 2004, I took a job at Providence St. Vincent Hospital. It was a good job with benefits that would support me while I made my decision. While working there, I started hearing little bits and pieces about music therapy, and it really sparked my interest. Even though I didn't know much about it, it seemed like such an amazing concept to me: using music to help people heal. I also heard that there was a music thanatologist who worked in St. Vincent Hospital, so I went in and talked to her about what she did. She explained to me the difference between music therapy and music thanatology, and she was very helpful in getting me thinking more about those areas of music. For a while, I wrestled with the possibility of becoming a music therapist and yet still wondered if I should stick to my original plan and just get my master's and teach, even though I knew that I felt no more called to it than I was before. Through all of this, another memory kept coming to me. During my last semester at college, I volunteered at an assisted living center for seniors. I helped out the activities coordinator and also sang for many of the residents. And I loved it. I left that place every time feeling completely fulfilled and blessed by those people. As I was struggling with career decisions, that place kept coming to my mind.

Finally, one day at work, I had what I like to call an epiphany. It was the smallest thing, but I still remember it so vividly. I was on my break and walking down the hall in radiology. There is an area in that hall where patients will sometimes be parked in their moving beds or wheelchairs, waiting to be taken up to their rooms. As I was walking by, I saw a little elderly woman in her bed all by herself, clutching her covers, just looking very sad and lonely. So I stopped to talk to her. We had a really nice conversation, and after a few minutes, she looked at me with tears in her eyes and said, "I wish that it was you that was taking me up to my room." I smiled at her and told her, "Well, I can't take you up to your room, but I will be happy to wait here with you until someone does come." And sure enough, a minute or so later, someone came to get her. As she was being wheeled away, she looked back at me and said, "Thank you so much for stopping."

As I continued to walk down the hall, I thought to myself how much those few minutes had just made my day. I had been able to help someone, even if it was in the smallest way, feel a little better, and it made me feel so blessed. And that is when I knew. I wanted to do that more. I wanted to do it every day, if I could. I loved helping people feel better, cheering them up, giving them a reason to be hopeful and happy, even while they are sick, alone, or afraid. Plus, there is a way to combine that with music, something else that I love and am passionate about! I just knew that it was what I wanted to do.

I still feel just as eager and excited to pursue this. When I talk to people about it and explain what music therapy is and what a difference it can make, I light up inside. I honestly don't know all that it entails or what I will be doing, but I know in my heart that I want to pursue this, and I am so excited!

*Megan Elliott works as a subcontractor with Earthtones Music Therapy Services in Portland, Oregon, specializing in work with older adults in a Parkinson's choir.*

# Chapter 4: Where Do Music Therapists Work?

The burning question often asked by prospective students (and sometimes parents, depending on whether the individual is traditional or nontraditional age in approaching a degree program) is this: What are the employment opportunities for a music therapist? Without any exaggeration, employment prospects for the music therapist are becoming plentiful. I frequently say that if you are willing to move from a particular locale, you will find work. New music therapy positions are becoming available on almost a weekly basis across the country. For the music therapy graduate, this is very good news!

## Schools

Depending on the state, music therapists will find employment in schools, particularly those with special education classrooms. They may assist or serve as the primary professional that works with children in need of special services. How many hours per week can be offered to the music therapist, whether in a full-time or part-time position, depends on the school's administration.

The children we most often serve are those with emotional or behavioral challenges and physical or developmental disabilities. Most recently, it has been discovered how successful music therapy is with those diagnosed with autism, and there is such a huge range of need.

Marie Durfee, who works with children on the autism spectrum, speaks to the communication factor about this disability: "Through music, these children who are all nonverbal are given a chance to communicate and interact...with music, they are more relaxed, and the pressure they are under at school and at home to speak is alleviated." Caleb Hastings addresses communication in his essay: "I have also learned that so much communication, possibly some of the most important communication, is nonverbal. Sometimes vocabulary and linguistics play no part in the connection with another person." Laetitia Lutts echoes a similar sentiment: "As a musician, I yearn to give everyone the chance to embrace this powerful yet simple form of communication." Jessica Western echoes the above: "Music is, to me, the most complete medium of communication."

It seems appropriate to present an experience a prospective music therapy student had about her sparks of interest in music therapy. Heather Delaney wrote the following in her essay:

> When I was in the fourth grade at Mount Scott Elementary School in Clackamas, Oregon, our class had two students from the special education classroom join us for reading time. I developed a close friendship with one of the boys named Warren, who had Down's syndrome. He was a joy to be around and always made me smile. I became close with his family and would go to movies with them and spend days during the summer swimming with Warren in his pool. This friendship went on through my sophomore year of high school… From this experience came a passion in my heart for disabled children and adults.

This culminated in Heather's application to the music therapy program.

## Medical Hospitals

Throughout the country, medical hospitals have started to enthusiastically use our services. In 2012, *Louisville Magazine* reported that about three hundred certified music therapists were working in hospitals throughout the United States, and forty-six of them were employed by hospitals in Kentucky.[1] With music therapy's increasing visibility, I suspect that in the years since that report those employment numbers have increased. Music therapists are used to address patient needs related to physical rehabilitation, pre- and postsurgical procedures, cardiac conditions, obstetrics, childbirth, chronic pain, diabetes, headaches, and other conditions. Research has shown that music decreases blood pressure, reduces stress hormones, and elevates hormones that impart a sense of well-being.

In a hospital, music may be used to enhance proper breathing techniques and promote relaxation for a patient with a weakened lung condition. It may be used as a positive distraction during procedures such as blood draws or vaccinations. Research has shown that some of the benefits of music include decreased blood pressure, reduced stress hormones such as cortisol (while elevating hormones that impart a sense of well-being), decreased need for pain medication, ease in building rapport between patient and medical personnel, and increased self-esteem.

Anne Vitort, a former Kindermusic early childhood educator, describes in her essay a hospital occurrence that led to her entrance into a music therapy program. Anne was offering a musical experience to a little girl with leukemia who had two IVs in her chest. "She and I, her mom, and the other visitors were parading around the room, each with an instrument in hand, playing and singing "Yankee Doodle" with abandon…Profoundly moved by the result of my amateur attempt at music therapy, I resolved to find out how and why music has such tremendous power."

Research and clinical experiences are showing music therapy's success with patients who may resist other treatment strategies in the medical setting. "Music is a form of sensory stimulation, which provokes responses due to the familiarity, predictability, and feelings of security associated with it."[2]

## Psychiatric Hospitals

Psychiatry was one of the first professions to realize the value of using music with patients who would otherwise not respond to various modalities of talk therapy. Since my internship days with the Milwaukee County Mental Health Complex (now known as the Milwaukee County Behavioral Health Division), and subsequently working on the in-patient psychiatric unit at Poudre Valley Hospital in Fort Collins, Colorado, I've experienced the value of music serving as a means of self-expression without words.

Jillian Hicks speaks to this in her essay:

> All of us have a desire and need to be heard and through music the restrictions of language dissipate...When people create music, they have a story to tell, a snippet of wisdom, a random thought, an emotion.

## Additional Mental Health Settings

Community mental health centers, drug and alcohol rehabilitation programs, and halfway houses have found our services invaluable for their clients' continuing recovery. They may simply maintain a quality of life that is otherwise unavailable to individuals suffering from mental health issues. I have often said to my students that it is much easier to see that someone with a bandaged arm or leg in a cast is in need of help, but how often do you see people with a cast around their head? They may be suffering from a mental health condition such as depression, anxiety, or obsessive compulsive disorder (OCD). How far does your compassion or understanding extend to these folks?

As music therapists, we ourselves often benefit from the use of music as therapy. Scott Garred echoes this in his essay: "Music has truly been therapy for me. It has helped me lift myself out of many bad times. It has helped me understand so much about my existence and my relationships with others."

The soulful service of a music therapist may be of immense help to folks struggling with a mental illness. Clients or patients may be more open to a musical alternative that enables them to express their feelings than a talk therapy approach. In the essay by an anonymous music therapist, we read, "I want to help kids and adolescents find their own voice and claim it and realize it is beautiful just as it is. I want to help others find that meaning that can't be expressed and continue to find my own."

## Correctional Facilities

In the 1980s, Dr. Michael Thaut was instrumental in establishing a music therapy protocol within Michigan's prison system, and he performed some groundbreaking research. The research was published in the AMTA's *Music Therapy Perspectives*.[3] Since then, correctional facilities have begun to recognize how music therapy helps inmates to improve their mood and attitude toward incarceration.

## Additional Agencies

Agencies serving individuals with developmental, hearing, or visual impairments are another source of employment for music therapists. As Emily Wiggins states, "I'm most fascinated by its effects on children with developmental disabilities. As I had a few handicaps to overcome in life, I'm of the firm belief that handicaps do not have to be disabling."

Dr. Kate Gfeller, director of music therapy at the University of Iowa, has been recognized for her work with patients of cochlear implants.

Gfeller authored seminal research surrounding cochlear implants in the 1980s and 1990s. As a result, the hearing impaired community has become more aware of the benefits of music therapy strategies. They are able to work through the challenges of the groundbreaking procedure.

## Senior Citizen or Retirement Centers

Senior citizen or retirement centers have long been aware of their residents' positive responses to music and the benefits of using music in their daily and weekly schedules. (Plato dictated that music be included in people's daily schedule.) Employing full-time music therapy services to benefit their clients is an adventure in these facilities. Music therapy colleagues around the country educate these facilities about the benefits of employing music therapists as opposed to putting on a CD, playing music on a radio, or hiring a musical entertainer for a monthly sing-along gig.

It has been a challenge to help the staff members understand the benefits of an approach that may seem like a sing-along but that includes a clinical approach. The clinical approach benefits individual needs, which the music therapist is trained to manage in a group setting. Even the most regressed resident taking part in an experience like a sing-along will benefit from music therapy.

## Assisted Living Homes

The plethora of assisted living homes that have sprung up in response to the aging baby boomer population accounts for another one of our many employment resources. These homes often require a higher degree of medical care for their residents. Music therapists targeting these facilities for employment can take training in rehabilitation and neurological music therapy approaches such as that offered at the Academy of Neurologic Music Therapy at Colorado State University.[4]

Training in neurological music therapy may enhance a music therapist's skill to accommodate the specific needs of the residents in these settings. As Keiko Shiokawa suggests in her essay, "I hope...as a neurologic music therapist to help people improve and recover from their brain damage through using music that can be a breakthrough tool." (Keiko is currently working as a neurologic music therapist in a rehabilitation hospital in Japan.)

Within these homes, the music therapist may be called upon to provide both individual and group experiences for the residents. Musical experiences will likely include a variety of approaches. Exciting rhythm ensembles, singing together, tone chime choirs, relaxation exercises, and "armchair tai chi" all inspire the creative spark necessary for a real quality of life. I found armchair tai chi to be fun, and it was highly accepted by the veterans I worked with at the Milwaukee County VA in Wisconsin.

Music therapists working full time in these settings will often be called upon to manage or facilitate other types of program experiences. It will fall under their job description to occasionally supervise outings or board games like Bingo for the residents. It is often a challenge to help staff understand the clinical nature of our profession's work, because in many areas of the country, we are new at providing services to this booming population. We find ourselves in a continual cycle of educating those we work with.

## Hospice Programs

Although we are just beginning to serve the needs of the hospice population, hospice programs are learning the value of employing music therapists to serve the desires of people on the threshold of transitioning from this reality. To meet the needs of the families and loved ones who are involved, the music therapist often includes the entire family. Music experiences such as listening to favorite songs of the transitioning client or active music making (such as singing with guitar, piano, or flute accompaniment) might be employed. All of this is done for the sake of the hospice clients and their loved ones.

Many young professionals may be drawn to hospice work as a direct or indirect result of the spiritual revolution sweeping the country. Addressing the spiritual needs of our planet's inhabitants seems to be of paramount interest to many of us; the spirit and soul issues are close to the heartbeat of every music therapist I have ever met. The desire to work on a one-on-one basis may be prompting new music therapists to take up the baton and address this special population.

Eric Hickey says the following: "As a music therapist, I have an interest in working with people of all ages who are in hospice care. A fear of death burdens some people for their entire lives, and I anticipate learning new ways of using music to help those nearing their death meet this end with a sense of tranquility."

Julie Ide shared the following: "With music therapy, I will be provided the chance to work closely with the elderly using music to meet their needs...I am open to working with all kinds of people but have a desire to work in a nursing home, hospital, or with hospice care."

## Wellness Programs

Given the health consciousness of seniors today and the fact that many folks are in compromised physical states, wellness program managers are realizing the importance of adding a skilled music therapist to their staff. Wellness led Kara Ryan into music therapy. As she says in her essay, "It is my passion for music, wellness, and people that leads me to pursue a career in music therapy."

Barbara Reuer, PhD, MT-BC, leads the Resounding Joy agency in the San Diego area and has established a noteworthy wellness program.

"Resounding Joy's mission is to promote social, emotional, physical, and spiritual well-being through music." A primary experience that Resounding Joy has offered since its start in 2004 is drumming with elders.[5]

## Rhythm Protocols

Since the early 1990s, rhythm has been emphasized by many music therapy professionals. They are aware of rhythm's effect on our bodies and the value of using rhythmic activities to easily and quickly engage people. My professional work included initiating Drums Not Guns, a violence-prevention pilot project, while teaching at Willamette University and working with homeless adolescents at the HOME Youth and Resource Center in Salem, Oregon.[6] I worked with David Knott (then a student and now a colleague employed by Children's Hospital in Seattle). We developed a rhythmic protocol to use with homeless and challenged youth. The weekly practice of creative drumming experiences with the youth resulted in increased attending and following directions, improvement in their ability to express themselves, and in general, a more positive attitude. All of these results occurred while involved in a "drum circle intervention." I recall the enthusiasm and playfulness of the youth involved. It calls to mind Ted Owen's essay and his words about drumming: "Coming home from school as a teenager and being able to sit behind a set of drums and purge many pent-up frustrations of adolescence was a natural way for me to take care of myself." I can't help but think that these adolescents were also purging their pent-up frustrations by drumming them out. This was a special project, and we were connected by the sound of the drum.

The Drums Not Guns pilot project morphed into the Drum Trail Project in early 2000. This project specifically targeted behaviorally and emotionally challenged youth in special education classrooms in

Portland, Oregon, and Vancouver, Washington. The classroom teachers reported that the drumming experiences with these children were positive:

> "When Subject C felt that he was getting angry, he would tell me that he needed to go to a quiet place so that he wouldn't say or do something to another child out of anger. I would like this project continued."
> "Subject E showed not one moment of oppositional behavior; he initiated a little more flexibility; no meltdowns (before these were apparent)."
> "The teachers have remarked that they are seeing (more) control among those students participating in the Drum Trail Project."
> "The kids are being more thoughtful in their writing, more reflective…perhaps as a result of them filling out those questionnaires pre and post session every week."

The teachers offered positive support for this project.

## Private Practice

Although there are many other places that employ our services throughout the country, the last example is the private contractual music therapist. The idea of being your own boss seems to be appealing in ways that music therapists may not have realized before.

In many areas of the country, you might be the only music therapist for hundreds of miles and have no choice but to start a private practice. Carla Carnegie provides this example in her essay:

I own and operate my private practice, Willow Song Music Therapy, where I serve individuals and groups living with developmental disabilities, autism, Parkinson's disease, dementia/Alzheimer's, well elders, and more. At this point, I travel to my clients, in the Spokane, Washington, Coeur d'Alene, and Post Falls, Idaho areas, providing treatment in their private home, assisted living facility, retirement facility, adult family home, resource center, and public community center. I also conduct workshops on stress management/wellness for the public, using music recreationally to benefit individual well-being. In the near future, Willow Song will be expanding to incorporate Music Therapy space shared with other therapies, to bring more access to individuals needing music therapy. Teaching music lessons on piano and violin for typically functioning individuals, and adaptive lessons for individuals needing a unique approach, rounds out my practice. Additionally, consulting, music notation/transcription services, playing in a band, and serving as a church pianist hones other skills as a musician.

Imagination and creative instincts drive professionals to explore how to contribute to the well-being of others and carve out a living for themselves. The combination of lessons and presenting music therapy possibilities to would-be employers offers the solo practitioner further opportunities to practice.

## Sample Job Description

The following is a typical job description for a contractual music therapist. In this case, an agency seeks a music therapist to provide a broad range of services to a varied population.

**Population**: Children and adolescents with autism and other individuals with developmental disabilities, e.g., dementia, mental health, substance abuse, adaptive music lessons, others.

**Start date**: Immediate.

**Description of position**: Growing private practice seeks a motivated, energetic, and independent music therapist to conduct group and individual sessions with a wide variety of populations. Allowances for continuing education, supervision, supplies, and instrument purchases are available.

While X-country skiing with my Shelties, always thinking about where we music therapists work!

# Essays

## Music Therapy Essay
## (Contributed by a music therapist who wished to remain anonymous)

"Music is the vernacular of the human soul."—Geoffrey Latham

I discovered my love of playing music the summer I was nine. As part of an arts camp I attended, I chose a percussion class on impulse. I had always loved dancing around to my dad's Motown records, but I knew nothing about playing an instrument.

The first day, I wandered into a room of adolescent boys hammering away at bongo drums. It was loud and sweaty and crazy. The coolest thing my tomboy heart had ever seen. The rhythm spoke to me.

I could not wait to get my own drum set. Drums became my joy, the song of my heart. I attended drum seminars, played in school bands, and beat away at my set for hours. I dreamed of a professional drumming career. Through percussion, I found a way to express all the energy bursting inside of me, an energy that sports or school or friends did not liberate. Music held a different place. (Speaking to the unique aspect of the power music brings in supporting the full expression of our humanness or musical intellect: "Play the music, not the instrument"—author unknown.)

Somewhere, things changed.

When I was fifteen, I began my struggle with depression and anxiety. We had moved to a small island three years earlier upon my mother's remarriage, and although I never quite felt like I fit in anywhere, it was not until my mid-teen years that the sense of isolation and loneliness seriously affected me. I developed severe acne, and my self-confidence plummeted. Taunts haunted me; my inflamed ugliness never left me. People terrified me. Their judgment and disapproval became my greatest fear. I was that girl who ate lunch in the bathroom.

I have always been a perfectionist, but I went to new lengths. Constantly aware of others' judgment of my appearance, I decided to shape my "worthiness" through my accomplishments. I linked my identity with my actions and talents; I was what I did. What I did was why people loved me. Therefore, what I did had to be perfect. I was an avid academic achiever; I was going to save the world; I was going to travel everywhere and do everything and help everyone. My life was impressive on paper, but my perfectionism stifled me. I couldn't breathe.

Crippling social anxiety and pressure claimed my life. Instead of flowing with the music, I rehearsed prefabricated drum patterns and mechanical fills for hours. Playing music in front of others became torture. I was so aware of others judging me that playing ceased to be joyful. Rarely did I let loose that creativity that once ignited me, because taking chances meant the possibility of messing up.

I practiced in my room day after day, like an automaton. What I played was not music, because there was no release, no emotion, no life. Playing with others was not a prospect. I could not. Eventually it became too lonely to have rhythm without melody, so I stopped playing altogether.

When I stopped expressing that part of me, something in me died. I lost my voice.

"The whole problem can be stated quite simply by asking, 'Is there a meaning to music?' My answer would be, 'Yes.' And 'Can you state in so many words what the meaning is?' My answer to that would be, 'No.'—Aaron Copland

Over the next few years, my life became a silent chaos. On the outside, my life seemed put together, glued by "impressive" accomplishments—academic accolades, admission to prestigious schools, travel to foreign countries. But I was dying inside. Naturally a passionate participator in life, I slowly drifted away from everything joyous as I become more involved in drugs and alcohol. Where music and life once stood, darkness took over. By the end of my first semester at Wesleyan University, life had spiraled out of control. I knew I needed help.

Thus began one of the most painful journeys: the healing process. I changed everything around me in order to rebuild my life. I moved out to California and successfully completed two drug and alcohol rehab programs. I built my life around my recovery. The community I found out there saved me, and for that I am eternally grateful.

It was there, at 3:00 p.m. every Saturday, that I realized the importance of reclaiming my voice.

The first time I walked into the Costa Mesa creative share recovery meeting, I knew I had found home. For an hour and a half, I sat among other sober addicts as they danced, sang, read poetry, and strummed away on guitars. That part inside of me that I had been so good at killing for the past few years felt alive again inside those four walls. No one cared about how good he or she was because it came from the heart. I had never heard so much life, and it had been a long time since I had really heard music.

I sat and listened for a few weeks, admiring everyone's creativity. I wanted to have what they had, do what they did. Something immense was missing from my life.

Then, one Saturday in August, the urge to go out and get a guitar overwhelmed me. I had to play music, or I was going to explode. An hour later, I purchased my first guitar.

When I started to play, words of pain, loss, growth, and gratitude poured forth. I focused on playing for me, not for others. I let my voice come out naked. I connected with that deeper part inside of my soul, not dots on a sheet of paper or perfect scales and impeccable rhythms. Creating something greater than myself played an integral part in the healing process. Delving back into music again that year, but with a different perspective than I played with before, led me to discover new opportunities.

I came across the field of music therapy this past year when a friend mentioned it to me. I had no idea such a profession existed. I researched it. The more I found out about the field, the more it made sense in my heart. I have always wanted to go into some therapeutic profession because of the bond I feel with people who struggle. In addition, I always knew there is a creative part of me that I yearn to express.

I wish there had been someone to comfort me through my anxiety and depression, to guide me on how to use percussion as an instrument of release instead of something at which I thought I had to be perfect. A mentor, who believed in my music ability, yet did not judge me for or become impatient of my anxiety disorder and depression.

I want to help kids and adolescents find their own voice and claim it and realize it is beautiful just as it is. I want to help others find that meaning that can't be expressed, and continue to find my own.

## Music Therapy Audition Essay
## Heather Delaney, MT-BC

My musical career started incredibly early in life. My performing debut was at church when I was three years old. My mother, sister, and I sang "Love in Any Language" by Sandi Patti and did sign language along with the song. My experiences in music go back to before I was even born. Without a doubt, my mother is the most influential musical figure in my life. She taught elementary school music for thirty-two years and has performed in choirs and as a soloist since a young age. What I have learned from my mom is not just all the technicalities but the expression—how to internalize music—and make it your very own. My love and passion for music has stemmed from hers, and I am so grateful to her.

My musical experience did not end at age three. At church, I was involved in choirs from second grade through my freshman year of college. During elementary school, we performed many different children's musicals. I was actively involved in all these performances. In the high school choir, we had the privilege to travel to California every summer to reach different churches and schools with our music ministry. I also had the opportunity to be involved in choirs at school. From fifth grade until now, I have been in a school choir every year. My freshman year of high school, I was in the sophomore-aged women's choir. At the end of the year, I received the award for "Most Valuable Singer" in the ensemble. Then my sophomore year, I was in the junior/senior level a cappella choir. I remained in this group for three years, serving as section leader for my junior and senior year, along with being a member of the advanced ensemble. My junior year we had the privilege of traveling to New York City to sing in Carnegie Hall with other groups from all over the United States; it was an amazing opportunity that we all enjoyed very much.

During my freshman year of college, while attending Mt. Hood Community College, I was in the advanced ensemble called the Chamber Singers. We traveled to Victoria, Canada, and I had a soprano solo that I was able to sing in an incredibly beautiful church from a high loft—it was an unforgettable experience. For the past two years, I have attended Seattle Pacific University and have been in the principal choir, the concert choir. We have traveled to Northern Washington, Idaho, and Southern California. Last year, I was also in the vocal jazz ensemble at SPU. Singing lead soprano, I was able to grow immensely in my vocal jazz skills as well as my solo and improvisational skills.

Undoubtedly my most rewarding choral experience was with the Portland Symphonic Girl Choir. It is a Portland metro area young women's choir directed by Roberta Q. Jackson. From sixth grade through my senior year of high school, I traveled all over the world with this amazing group of girls. In the summer of 1995, we went to Italy and sang in St. Peter's Cathedral. We traveled to Australia in 1997 and to Scotland and England in 2000. Because of this choir, I have experienced much more of the world than I ever could have dreamed.

With all of this musical background and passion, it would seem logical for me to be a music teacher or even a vocal performance major, but my heart seemed to lie in a slightly different place, and I wasn't exactly sure where. When I was in the fourth grade at Mt. Scott Elementary School in Clackamas, Oregon, our class had two students from the special education classroom join us for reading time. I developed a close friendship with one of the boys named Warren, who had Down's syndrome. He was a joy to be around and always made me smile. I became close with his family and would go to movies with them and spend days during the summer swimming with Warren in his pool. This friendship went on through my sophomore year of high school when unfortunately, due to behavioral reasons, Warren had to be sent to a different school. From this experience came a passion in my heart for disabled children and adults. Spring term of my freshman year of college, I was in a writing class that required a research paper to be written over the course of the term. We could pick any topic we wanted, and I chose music education and special education.

One day while I was in the library doing some research on my topics, I came across a journal entry on music therapy. At the time, I had never heard of music therapy, and out of curiosity, I kept reading. It discussed the goals of music therapy, who it is for, and what it has and is accomplishing. At that moment, I knew this was what the Lord had in store for my future, and it was the "slightly different thing" that I wanted to do with my life. I changed the topic of my paper to music therapy and was able to study it for the remainder of the term, each day falling more in love with the idea.

For the past two years, I have been involved in a ministry called Young Life Open Door for disabled teens. We meet once a week for a "club" where we sing songs, play games, and the kids have an opportunity to hear about Jesus. I have led music occasionally for the group; we sing secular songs that the kids know as well as some simple worship songs. I have gained some amazing friendships with the students in Open Door, and I can honestly say this will be the hardest thing for me to leave at the end of the year.

I first heard about Marylhurst University through a friend of mine. After I had mentioned the desire to receive my master's in music therapy, she shared her knowledge of Marylhurst's program. When I went online to research the master's program, I found there was only a four-year degree available. I immediately discussed it with my mom, and we realized that the best option would be to finish my four-year degree at Marylhurst rather than getting my general music degree from Seattle Pacific and then trying to find a school with a master's in music therapy. This led me to contacting the school, ultimately contacting Christine Korb, and arranging my audition for the program. I am very excited to begin this amazing journey to my career in which I find such passion—I couldn't ask for a better combination.

*Heather Delaney, MT-BC, sings in the Portland Choral Arts Ensemble.*

## Communicating through Music
## Marie Durfee, MT-BC

Nina* marches around her classroom holding a blue wooden cylinder in each hand. She is marching to a beat only she can hear, and at age four and a half, she keeps a fairly steady rhythm. "Wushuvabuhbee are you okay?" exclaims Nina.

She has been repeating the same line since I met her at the bus five minutes earlier, one of several scripts she says throughout the day. Her long brown hair shakes over her backpack as she turns her head left and right in rhythm with her steps. "Wushuvabuhbee are you okay?" she says again, her pale arms pumping up and down as she circles around the small classroom.

"Nina, backpack off," I say as I walk toward her. "Let's hang it up."

Nina continues to march though changes direction so that now she is heading away from me, string bean legs moving up and down over feet that point inward. Transition times are especially difficult for children with autism, and Nina is no exception.

I move ahead of her and squat to her level. Her big gray eyes refuse to meet mine as she stomps her feet and swings her arms in place. "Nina," I say as her head moves back and forth and the wooden blocks bounce in from on my face, "let's take backpack and jacket off." I stand and ask for the blocks saying "my turn" as I remove them gently from her little hands and place them on a cabinet. Holding her hand, I begin to lead her to her cubby.

Immediately she pulls her hand from mine, arms go straight up in the air, and she begins to scream. "Wushuvabuhbee are you okay?" she cries and then screams again in a pitch so high my ears ring as she brings her fists down once on top of her head.

I pause for a minute to let her calm herself and then repeat the direction. "Nina, backpack and jacket off first, then play time."

This time she allows me to lead her to her cubby and goes through her morning routine as I give her verbal cues. "Backpack off, hang it up," then "jacket off, put it in," I say as I tap her cubby. Once her jacket is in her cubby, I unzip her backpack, and we go through the last couple directions of taking out her lunch and placing it in the lunch basket. "Great job, Nina, you can play." She walks over to the table and picks up two new wooden cylinders, this time both red, and begins to march in big circles around the room.

I offer Nina markers and paper or the number puzzle she loves so much in an attempt to engage her. She is not quite ready to attend, and I allow her to march for a couple minutes as her classmates arrive, and I hear "Spencer, backpack off," "Josey, backpack off," "Sam, backpack off." After they've all had a few minutes to play around the room, they are handed a poker chip and told to check their schedules. I take the blocks from Nina and hand her the chip. Arms go straight up, and the screaming begins again. "Nina, let's check your schedule. It's circle time!" Circle time is her favorite time, yet she continues to scream as she walks over, drops the poker chip in the cup next to her picture schedule, and pulls off the picture of circle time. For children with autism, transitions are extremely difficult, and Nina especially has a hard time.

As she walks to circle, I sing the "circle time" song, "Circle time, circle time, everybody knows it's circle time." She quiets herself and carries her Velcro circle time picture over to the circle area and tucks the picture into its corresponding envelope. Nina chooses a seat and waits patiently for teacher Debbie to begin circle. An aid sits behind each child, and we begin with a song. "Well hello everybody and how are you? How are you? How are you?" By the second "you," Nina is joining in and saying "you." She is looking directly at Debbie and smiling as she sings that one little word with us. When we slow the song down drastically, Nina will also say "hah wah you" for "how are you."

On most days, Nina remains engaged through all of circle time so long as we are singing or playing music. Without either, she withdraws back into her world of scripting as she repeats lines or laughs at something only she can know. Nina is not unlike her classmates who also come alive, making eye contact and smiling during circle time while we sing and play music. Teacher Debbie holds up two books that go along with two songs, "Baby Beluga" and "Chica Chica Boom Boom." She waits for one of the four children to either point or make a sound to indicate which book we will sing. All four sets of eyes stare eagerly at Baby Beluga, and we sit back and wait to see who will request it. Nina's eyes are huge and filled with excitement; she rocks back and forth as she looks at the book. After a brief moment, Sam emits a "bah bah" and points to Baby Beluga. Debbie starts the CD player, and all four kids move to the music in their seats and watch the pages intently, occasionally reaching their little hands toward the book when Debbie doesn't turn the pages quick enough to stay with the music.

For twenty minutes, Nina has been attentive and smiling. In that time, she experiences something every four-year-old should have access to constantly throughout the day: connection with another person. Circle time is one of the only places where Nina will talk; the other place is in the "green room." The green room is a pivotal response training (PRT) room where I work and play with Nina every day. In this room, I kneel in front of Nina while she sits in her chair and try to interest her with various toys I have with me. The goal is to get a sound or sign language from her, which will be immediately rewarded by a minute or two of playing with the toy.

"Nina," I say and wait until she looks at me, "xylophone." I sing and then play the eight notes and again sing, "Xylophone," stretching the word out slowly. Nina smiles, and her big eyes meet mine as if to say "Now you're speaking my language." For eye contact I reward her with the xylophone. She plays each note, looks at me, and says, "Xylophone." The first time this happened, tears flooded my eyes, and it was all I could do not to completely fall apart right then and there. Since then, she will say this every time I take out the xylophone, sing "xylophone," and play the eight notes. For those few minutes she is able to leave the comfort of her world and enter the overwhelming classroom to share this time with me. She is able to find pleasure and encouragement in interacting with another person. She smiles and laughs and looks right into my eyes. For those few minutes, the scripting stops, and she watches me carefully as we take turns playing the xylophone. Nina only has a few words, and one of them is xylophone. Through this small instrument, we are communicating.

To Nina's frustration, it has taken me a while to pick up on her language, but I am working at it, and I can tell she understands this. I have a song for keeping shoes on at school, a song for going in from recess, and many more little transition songs. Most of them have a similar tune, but she doesn't mind unless I sing out of key, and then she lets me know pretty quickly with a frown (and occasionally a yell) that that is not okay with her. Nina is not alone either; her classmates respond amazingly to music and also do not hesitate to let me know they disapprove of my singing out of key. Through music, these children who are all nonverbal are given a chance to communicate and interact. A few hum songs constantly throughout the day and will smile and meet my eyes whenever I join them. With music, they are more relaxed, and the pressure they are under at school and at home to speak is alleviated. Therefore, it is during circle time, when we are singing, that words or sounds will come out to request a song or join in singing. Their faces will light up with the small amount of control they feel over their young lives with the utterance of a word or sound.

Four hours have passed, and it is time to bring the children to their buses. "Goodbye Nina, goodbye Nina, goodbye Nina, we're glad you came today," I sing. Nina instantly goes to her schedule with her poker chip, plunks it in the chip cup, and peels off the Velcro bus picture. She walks over to her cubby as a couple of her classmates join in the goodbye song by humming as they put on their jackets and backpacks. Nina smiles up at me as I sing, fully understanding that this song signifies the end of the day. I sing "Hold my hand to walk to the bus, walk to the bus, walk to the bus" similar to the tune of "Wheels on the Bus," and Nina reaches up and puts her little hand in mine. Together we walk down the ramp as I sing the goodbye song, and Nina bounces along beside me.

* Names have been changed for reasons of confidentiality.

*Marie Durfee works as a contractual music therapist, serving individuals on the autism spectrum.*

## My Music Therapy
## Scott Garred, MT-BC

Music is quite often what people turn to when despair settles in. Many times life's little challenges are too much to handle on one's own. These challenges, big and small, can be handicapping. Music is therapy. We see and hear music working in a variety of ways. It's something turned up loud when one simply has a bad day. It's something that can be added to a person's life that might be caught in some kind of struggle, perhaps with societal issues. It's in our environment by way of a cool breeze whistling through the trees. Maybe it's just a simple tune a man or woman hums while leaving a stressful day at the office. Maybe the day is not stressful at all, and the song is reinforcing one's soul and happiness.

And, for me, well, I feel good when I pick up a guitar, strum the simplest of chords, and sing a tune. Usually it is a sad tune, but it is the sort of tune that makes me happy. In this way, music becomes therapy for me. Music is in my soul. And in my opinion, it needs to be in all people. At the very least, it's worth trying.

It all started when I was in the fifth grade. I thought it was cool to visit with the pep band at junior high basketball games, just sitting and letting the trumpets clean out my ears.

Upon entering the sixth grade, I started playing the trumpet in band and taking guitar lessons across town from a man whose name I have forgotten but whose teaching I will never forget. He instilled in me not scales and methodology but chords—the simplest of chords. The first ones I learned were, in this order, G, G7, D7, and C. "Don't come back until you know these chords!"

My first guitar was something I still own today, a Global acoustic. It's some boxy old thing my mom had. She sang, "Will the spearmint lose its flavor on the bed post overnight? When you chew it in the morning, will it snap right back and bite?" Probably on the same four chords I still play today. They are, in this order, G, G7, D7, and C.

I went back the following week. I played the chords while my teacher picked out the melodies. Sometimes he played the banjo. Then he might say, "Let me tune that wretched thing." Then we'd switch after a while, and I would pick for a spell. I was his best student, or so he would say. I went back after each summer for three years. That is until my ninth grade year—I was told he passed on. I continued lessons in the same mom and pop store only with a different teacher. I was probably his best student too, but it wasn't the same.

All this time, I continued trumpet in the concert band. I made sure I was first chair or at least in a position to challenge it. I remember my first trumpet—a shiny silver King. I later sold it for a camera. I'll explain that later. I also began playing guitar in the jazz band. The chords I had never heard of before! My band teacher was patient with me though. He provided me with a chord book for jazz guitar. In it, I looked up these strange chords the night before we played a new piece. Just trying to imagine my fingers above the seventh fret was quite a feat. By the time ninth grade came around, I was sight reading my way through a variety of stuff, dragging triplets everywhere and never discriminating against a chord even if it was diminished. We even performed as a "big band," playing classics such as "Take the A Train" for the locals to dance to.

But I was young, and I did have other interests. Besides, my high school music teacher made us march, and I couldn't stand that or the "band moms" who accompanied us to all those competitions across the state. My band teacher would not be where he is today, with one of the top band programs in the state, had I continued blaring blatantly wrong notes at the judges. Truth be told, I never learned a single marching band piece. I was a rebel with a skateboard, discovering punk rock and art, specifically photography. And I learned everything I could about photography until I became the only photographer on the newspaper and yearbook staff. It was so much work for one person that they decided to hire an advisor and pay me. I thought that was pretty good.

And what do you know? My advisor was quite a character to say the least. He was a retired photojournalist working out of his own lab restoring old photos. He was a Vietnam War veteran and a martial arts expert. He played guitar and became my biggest influence as a young person. He saved me from going down the same road twice, about to sell my electric guitar for another camera. He also introduced me to one of my all-time favorite singers and songwriters, Neil Young. You know what else? The chords sounded awfully familiar. Oh so soothing to me.

I had been away from music my sophomore and junior years of high school. But as a senior, aided by my photography advisor, I was at least interested again. Still, though, I needed a little something extra.

I got that something extra when a bass player friend of mine from college asked me to play some guitar with him. I helped him write out a jazz chart. We went over to a friend's house, a drummer from my high school, and jammed it out. I was playing again, but it wasn't right. It was that jazz stuff again. We could only "return to coda" so many times. Eventually we became sidetracked and switched gears completely. My friend taught me something I have never forgotten. We played D, A, and G with a rock beat. Over and over again, and he showed me how to solo on the G string, leaving the D open and ringing out constantly. I was floored. That same amp I used in jazz band actually played something I could understand and relate to. We were playing something completely original. A simple song formed, and I felt so alive. If my math teacher could have showed me these types of sine waves, I might be doing something else today. We played that song over and over again, at least once a month for most of my senior year. It never got old. The seed had been planted thanks to those early jam sessions. I was playing the same old chords with a new approach. I finally learned what my guitar teacher was trying to teach me: I found my soul in the music. And it's been something I have carried with me the last ten years of living. It has helped me believe in myself in all areas of life. I call that therapy.

I went to college up the road in another town, in a place I had been going regularly for the last several years to skateboard and listen to the punk bands that populated the community. I went to college there because I wanted to take my guitar and be a part of the scene.

My first order of business was to start a band. My second order of business was to get a degree. So I started a band and began my degree in communications. That was the closest my school had to a photography degree. From the beginning, I was directed by music and the feeling I got when I played with other people, live and in the same room. It was so different than band in junior high and high school. We rocked out for several years, released some music in the seven-inch 45 RPM format, and even landed an opening slot for a very popular British act called Echo and the Bunnymen.

I discovered the multitrack cassette recorder my senior year of college. I would graduate soon, and all I had learned was the minimum requirement to get my degree and a three-point-something-or-other grade point average and how to write and record a song complete with verse, chorus, verse, guitar solo, and end it, wrapped up tight. I thought I knew it all at that point. I closed my guitar case to preserve my melodies and left school with my BA in communications.

"Please mom, get me down from the car seat, I just turned twenty-two." Super XX Man Vol. I (*This is a line from Scott's song, speaking metaphorically about his journey to Austin, Texas, following graduation.*) She did, and a friend of mine and I landed in Austin, Texas. I had no idea it was the so-called "live music capital of the world."

And I guess it is in a way. It has been mine. I worked an odd photo lab job to a dead-end other job playing in my newly formed band, Silver Scooter.

At the same time, I started releasing my solo four-track stuff under the name Super XX Man. It was at my first photo lab job that I used to cry my eyes out. I would lock myself in the darkroom, turn on some music, and just cry. "What have I done?" I wondered. "Why have I moved here? Why have I left all of my old friends?" In the evenings, I would just write and write, interrupted only by depression. Music poured out of me. I recorded it, produced it, and sang my heart outside in every chance I could get. In September, I gave myself until December and then I would go back home to mom. The kid who graduated from college with all the answers was stuck between a rock and a hard place. It was under the influence of rock that he found something eventually.

Hundreds of songs and six Christmases later, I'm still here. I've released six volumes of music as Super XX Man, three full-length, critically lauded albums, and numerous singles and compilation tracks with Silver Scooter. With both musical projects, I have toured the United States a dozen or so times. I'll be returning to Japan next month with Silver Scooter for the second time.

Currently, I work as a freelance recording engineer, helping other bands and songwriters realize their potential. I'm working on Super XX Man Vol. VI, a concept album about a man searching for answers big and small. I love my work and what I have to show for it.

Music has truly been therapy for me. It has helped me lift myself out of many bad times. It has helped me understand so much about my existence and my relationships with others. It's helped a kid getting out of college to find life and lots of it as an adult. Perhaps I am now ready to be a music therapist or a teacher, helping others realize their potential to do great things.

*Scott Garred is currently working on a master's degree in counseling in Melbourne, Australia.*

## Music Therapy Entrance Essay
## Caleb Hastings, MT-BC

People will tell you that there are only two real subjects in whom an actual prodigy can exist: music and mathematics. Some will even go as far as to say that music is basically math and that the two are similar enough to be combined. The thought that someone could perform well beyond his or her own reasonable parameters is a testament to the natural human connection with music. This is the first factor that has sparked my interest in music therapy. With legitimate research in the areas of insomnia, depression, postsurgery anxiety, children with developmental problems, and autism, music is a therapeutic language for many sufferers of many conditions. Considerable improvement has been shown in all of these cases, which means that there is certainly a demographic with a need for music therapists.

Having suffered from insomnia for many years, I can empathize quite strongly with people who experience many of these problems, and

I have a personally vested interest in future research involving music therapy.

Being a musician born of English and speech teachers, strong communication with others has been a requisite to all aspects of my life. Productive and efficient communications benefit every situation in modern America. I have also learned that so much communication, possibly some of the most important communication, is nonverbal. Sometimes vocabulary and linguistics play no part in the connection with another person.

Going back to the idea of prodigy, the expression of music can cross social boundaries that speaking cannot, and this is another reason that I am so interested in the study of music therapy. Playing original music and traveling to share it with others has shown me the power and need for music no matter the location or situation; music will have a strong prevalence in my life no matter what I do. After completing an internship in Los Angeles, a place many would call a Mecca of sorts in the music industry, I also learned that commercial music is becoming a much more difficult industry to succeed in. Creativity and originality are quite rarely rewarded in the ways that they deserve. Using music as a conduit to better others and myself seems the best use of my skills. Since music therapy is a relatively young industry, I believe great advancements will be made in what we know about music therapy and the many uses it may have in the coming years. It is very exciting to think that I could have a part in extending the current knowledge about the uses of music therapy.

Out of all the places to study music, Oregon is at the top of my list. In the name of music, I have done a fair amount of traveling in the last few years. I have learned that the places with more art- and music-savvy populations are places that are the most conducive to advancements in both areas. I also believe that this environment will be one of the many places to foster the growth of music therapy because of its willingness to foster the growth of music. Learning skills in an area where I will be most likely to apply them sounds like a great use of my efforts. Being from Nebraska, I have developed a very innate need for natural beauty as well, and Oregon is a force to be reckoned with as far as landscape that is easy on the eyes. Combining an artistically accepting population with some of the most spectacular landscapes in America is an equation that will work well for me, as they are both elements that will keep me productive and ambitious.

Playing and writing music have been hallmarks of my life throughout and preceding my undergraduate education. From the most informal coffee shop to regional blues festivals, the most classless dive bars around, and a full-on orchestra performance, music is something that commands involvement and attention no matter what the audience, and I have experienced this firsthand.

I have practiced and played within many different dimensions of music. Formally learning jazz guitar showed me the rewards of concrete goals being attained through artistic practice. Music is something that requires structure and spontaneity, formality and creativity. Harnessing both the logical and emotional is something that has great potential for many people and has yet to be explored to the fullest.

In summary, my personal experiences and inclinations all point me toward music therapy. My attraction to music, communication, Oregon, and the advancement of therapy in so many different areas tells me that Marylhurst is the place for me. In comparison to other potential places to continue my education, every staff or faculty member I have spoken with, via email or telephone, has been quite supportive of my situation and all of my questions. In my opinion, the impression that comes out of the first few phone calls to a prospective school that occur with someone you have never met says a lot about the atmosphere of the institution itself. The helpful, friendly "vibe" that one gets from an interested and attentive front desk employee is indicative of a positive and productive environment overall. I like the sound of everything I have heard from or about Marylhurst University. This, met with my first love of music and the excitement of being involved in an industry with legitimate worth to myself and others, especially one that encompasses all of my interests and skills, the decision to study music therapy seems like a no-brainer.

*Caleb Hastings is now employed at Cincinnati Children's Hospital in Cincinnati, Ohio.*

## Let Go
### Jillian C. Hicks, MA, MT-BC

He walked in hesitantly with a nervous gait, violin case clenched in his fingers.

"Hi, I'm Jillian," I said as I greeted him with an outstretched hand.

"Ben, Ben Weinstein," he nervously stated.

I shook his sixty-year-old, weathered hand and offered him a seat.

Shifting with quick, jerky mannerisms, Ben remained standing. "So I've tried this violin thing, and I'm terrible. I don't know about this, but I really love the way violin music sounds. What do you do with this bow thing anyway? I have these books, and I tried this song, but it sounded awful."

This was our beginning. Over the next four months, I taught Ben every week. During our first lessons together, Ben would pace the room, sit, play a song, and whisper under his breath about how ugly the music he created was. He was convinced that he would never produce beauty. His lack of confidence was deeply rooted, and as our lessons progressed, I pondered where it had originated.

At each lesson, I would ask Ben to talk for a few minutes about how his week of practice had gone. Some weeks were better than others, but each was filled with many ups and downs. His playing was stiff and forced. In order to help him understand that music is an avenue of expression, we started doing breathing exercises and discussing how his self-deprecation was hindering his joy of playing.

As we continued working together, Ben began to play beautifully. His sound was effortless, and we both started to hear him progress. Laughter accompanied his songs. His personal story and voice began to develop. One week Ben told me the catalyst to taking up violin lessons had been a result of getting laid off from his job of thirty years. His sense of self-worth had completely escaped him at the time, and through playing, he was starting to get it back. I also learned he had lived in Israel, fought in the Vietnam War, and was a proud grandfather. By the end of the sixteen weeks, Ben had found a job and was moving to Arizona. During his last lesson, he gave me a card that read, "What you taught me is that music happens when you let go." His words were an affirmation of my own sense of self-worth.

The daily interactions I have had with my violin and fiddle students have motivated me toward an interest in music therapy. Seeing firsthand what music has done to increase the self-confidence, inner exploration, higher understanding of self, and healing in each of my students has been a powerful influence on this life venture. Being a part of this process has made teaching the most rewarding and challenging work that I have done. There is something inherently grounding and freeing when music is created or heard. When people create music, they have a story to tell, a snippet of wisdom, a random thought, an emotion. All of us have a desire and need to be heard, and through music, the restrictions of language dissipate.

Currently, I feel limited in my abilities to use music as a therapeutic tool, because I have not yet had the opportunity to learn the skills provided by a degree in music therapy. To be able to work with people in a clinical setting where direct interactions, assessments, and treatment plans are used in tandem with music is where my interests are growing. As I was able to experience with Ben, music contains the possibilities for change, healing, and growth, which are seemingly endless.

*Jillian Hicks is now employed with Willamette Valley Hospice in Salem, Oregon.*

## Music Therapy: Using My Talent and Passion for a Healing Purpose
## Julie Ide, MT-BC

When I first began my freshman year at Seattle Pacific University, I was uncertain of what degree I wanted to pursue. I chose to start out as an intended nursing major. Not because I loved the idea of being a nurse but because it seemed like a very practical career field that would fit with my personality. It felt good to know exactly what I was doing and what my goal would be by pursuing this degree. But I was continually feeling very uncertain and unconvinced that this was the right path for me. My first interest, talent, and passion was music.

I have always been extremely involved in singing from the time I was in the third grade. I have been in a choir since I can remember. I have participated in many solo vocal competitions and have received numerous awards. I have also participated in musical theater, playing the eldest daughter in *Fiddler on the Roof.* I have been very involved in my church, singing on the worship team and occasionally in the choir. I have spent the last four years participating in my university's select concert choir and in a small select contemporary Christian worship band on campus. All of these experiences have shaped the person and vocalist that I am today, for which I'll be forever grateful. For some of these reasons, it was hard to make much sense of becoming a nurse. I was also interested in being music major or even possibly a theology major but was having a hard time convincing myself of the practicality of these. Should I do something I might absolutely love and be excellent at or something I might be quite good at that would provide very well? This was the looming question.

After much prayer, thought, and many conversations, I decided to begin classes for the music major at Seattle Pacific. However, I continued to complete some of the core requirements for nursing in case I decided to pursue it. Around this time is when I heard about the possibility of doing music therapy. I heard mention of it a few times, but it now began to sink in as a reality.

I realized that music therapy would combine my love of and talent for music with my ability to be compassionate, empathetic, and gentle with people. It would also give me a path to follow for a stable career while pursuing a degree in music. I decided to officially declare myself as a general music major at Seattle Pacific University. I realized that there was no music therapy program in place, but I found that Marylhurst University, close to my home, had an excellent program. At the time, I wasn't sure exactly how it would all work out, but I knew that I could not leave Seattle at this time. It was truly where I was supposed to be.

In hearing more and more about music therapy, I have realized why I want to become a music therapist and why it fits so well. Sometime during the first part of my college career, I began to understand that there is a great need for the elderly to be cared for, listened to, helped, and healed. Before I knew that I would pursue music therapy, a passion for this population of people was stirred in me. With music therapy, I will be provided the chance to work closely with the elderly using music to meet their needs. I am open to working with all kinds of people but have a desire to work in a nursing home, hospital, or with hospice care. It seems perfect to me now to combine my passion for music and helping people with my given personality and talents. It also enables me to utilize the classes I have already taken. Because I was thinking of nursing, I have taken courses such as anatomy and physiology (one of the toughest courses at Seattle Pacific), organic and biological chemistry, psychology, and child developmental psychology. Some of these courses, along with the extensive music courses, have given me a great foundation for music therapy.

I want to pursue music therapy not only because it fits my interests and skills, but it also fits very well with who I am (my personality strengths). Some of my strengths are listening, showing compassion, being empathetic, patient, gentle, and kind, and having a genuine interest in people.

I continue to receive confirmation from various people and experiences that music therapy is an excellent choice for me. I would love to have the opportunity to attend Marylhurst University and pursue this field of education in order to receive a second bachelor's degree in music therapy. I truly want to use what God has given me to meet this deep need for healing in the world through music therapy.

*Julie Ide works as a subcontractor for Earthtones Music Therapy Services in Portland, Oregon.*


## Music Therapy Essay
## Laetitia Lutts, MT-BC

Music is often referred to as the one true universal language. Throughout the ages, it has been considered one of the most influential factors in every society and culture. Even in its most rudimentary forms, music has a way of affecting lives in unlimited ways.

Ever since I was a young girl, I have been fascinated with music, playing and singing every chance I could. I took on the endeavor of teaching myself how to read music and play the piano, and since then, I have never stopped loving everything about this beautiful and mesmerizing art. I have always known that music would be a strong factor in my life, but I couldn't seem to figure out how. That is until I came upon the subject of music therapy. Personally, music has always been therapeutic. The feeling of peace and relaxation that comes from simply playing or listening to a piece of music is incredible. For some, simply the idea of music can help them through a difficult time.

Connections made through music come far and wide. Whether it comes from two strangers who meet jamming at an open mic night or a teacher giving his/her knowledge to a student, music has a way of binding people together. Music does not discriminate. It embraces all humanity, giving all of us a chance to connect in some way. When music becomes a factor, a new understanding and respect for life is found. As a musician, I yearn to give everyone the chance to embrace this powerful yet simple form of communication.

The first time that I was amazed at the powers that lie within music therapy was when I picked up the arts section of the *Boston Globe* and read an article about a ten-year-old boy who was a professional jazz pianist. Not only was he incredibly young, he was autistic as well. This may be a rare case, but the fact that it helped one autistic child communicate with the world makes me all the more hopeful that it could help millions more.

Through music therapy, this dream can become a reality. Even as a relatively new field (in the clinical sense), music therapy has consistently helped to improve the quality of life for many disabled and/or troubled people. A friend of mine works as a nurse in a rehabilitation facility, and even without an on-site music therapist, they use music to help relax their patients. She once said to me, "Sometimes it seems like nothing will reach a patient, and then we put on a certain song, and they finally open up and free their emotions. Sometimes a song will even move them to tears." Once more, music serves as a factor in helping someone through a difficult period.

Musicians can be found on any block, but few attempt to make a real difference through their music. Personally, one of my aspirations has always been to take music beyond its entertainment value and truly affect people in ways that could change their lives. Although I do not have that much experience in the field, I have found that its presence is not only necessary but also something in which I want to be involved. Everyone is given a chance to be the best person that they can be, and I feel that this is my calling. I can only hope that Marylhurst University will give me the opportunity to fulfill my dreams as a musician and as a human being.

*Laetitia Brundage is self-employed as a music therapist. As an independent contractor, she has worked for the Manchester Community Music School, the LABBB Educational Collaborative, and Groovy Baby Music. Her expertise is working with individuals with developmental disabilities in both group and one-on-one settings.*

## Why Music as Therapy, Not Performance?
## Keiko Shiokawa, MT-BC

Studying and eventually practicing music therapy is an integrated form of my love, interest, and hope for music.

**Love.** I started self-teaching piano since around four or five, hearing my sister practicing the piano and being motivated by it. However, my parents were reluctant to have me take lessons since all of my older sisters quit their lessons a few years after they started lessons. I was ten when my parents finally allowed me to take lessons. Although their decision was made later than I hoped, they were right: I still play the piano at the age of twenty! My other music background includes playing the euphonium, a wind instrument which looks like a baby tuba, through middle and high school, directing and conducting my school choirs and wind ensemble, and learning classical singing.

When I had to decide on a career path at the age of eighteen, at which Japanese young people take entrance exams of universities that consequently determine their career paths, I thought I couldn't live with any career not related to music.

**Interest.** I was fortunate not only to play the euphonium in the wind ensemble but also to have the opportunities to conduct it and chorus groups in my schools. Those experiences of organizing and integrating multiple players as one led me to be aware how strongly music can influence people's cognition…the power of music that keeps a group of seventy players together as one. Thinking back to those days, I am sure the awareness was the very starting point of my idea of "using" music for something else but performance.

In my last year at my high school, I encountered a book discussing interesting connections between music and language in the brain. Even though one lost his ability to talk due to the damage to parts of his brain, he can still "learn" to speak with singing—because singing uses his non-damaged brain areas of the brain. As the conducing experiences taught me, this book also taught me another side of music as a possible tool to help people recover from speech problems. If we turn the power of music into therapeutic use, what will happen?

**Hope.** I thought it would be a good idea to be a speech therapist and use music in my practice, so I went to observe a rehabilitation hospital for brain injured patients where speech therapists worked. I still can remember clearly the two patients who generously had me observe their speech therapy sessions. One lady was practicing to remember and say general materials names such as telephone, car, and book, but she was repeatedly saying her daughter's name. The speech therapist was so patient to continue asking the same questions. "What is this? Can you please name this?" But it looked to me so painful for the patient and the therapist. I met another male patient with swallowing difficulties due to his traumatic brain injury. He could not move most of his body parts, but he was clearly showing interest in the pudding placed at a corner of the tray. I heard he hit his head after getting drunk. He had worked just like other young men until three days before I met him. I was totally shocked by seeing these two patients struggling with their symptoms because of their brain injuries. They didn't hope to have those damages at all, but they got so unfortunately. Who does not have to help these people? Especially if you have ideas and skills that could help them more effectively and warmly, for example, through music.

After doing researching around my ideas, using music as a tool for rehabilitation for people with brain injuries, I have found that the United States is the pioneer in the area having cultivated the field of music therapy. In the United States, they have a specialized practice for brain-related symptoms called neurologic music therapy.

I hope to enter Marylhurst University's music therapy program and eventually become certified as a music therapist and also as a neurologic music therapist to help people improve and recover from their brain damage through using music that can be a breakthrough tool.

PS: Almost six years have passed since I wrote this essay. Now I have completed a four-year program at Marylhurst University and full-time internship. I have finally become an MT-BC, and I am currently working as a neurologic music therapist in a rehabilitation hospital in Japan.

**Music Therapy Essay**
**Anne Vitort, MBA, MT-BC**

A friend's daughter, whom I shall call "B" to protect her privacy, was undergoing treatment at Doernbecher Children's Hospital for leukemia. Her family had been part of my Kindermusik program; older brother "M" attended my classes for several years, and I was well acquainted with the parents and other family members. So when I was asked to visit "B" and her mom "J" at Doernbecher and bring some of my instruments, of course I did. I had not seen "B" in some time, and her appearance was typical for a leukemia patient: only a few tufts of hair remained, her face puffy, eyes gray. She had two IVs hooked into her chest and was not able to travel very far without needing to pull the pole along with her. I was told that during other visits, she was usually quite tired and listless, conversing only a little with visitors, so I didn't expect much.

I knew "B" liked animals, so I started singing a hello song followed by "The Bear Went over the Mountain" and "Five Bears Out Tonight." Soon she was singing with me and asked if she could see what instruments I had brought. She loved picking out melodies on my step bells, banging loudly on my hand drums and shaking my egg shakers with excited vigor. In short order, she and I, her mom, and the other visitors were parading around the room, each with an instrument in hand, playing and singing "Yankee Doodle" with abandon.

What was it that transformed this little girl, if only for a few moments, from a seriously ill child to a happy and carefree musician? How could a few moments of singing and music making release a little girl from the pain and frustration of hospital confinement? (I was told later that she had not been that animated since she had begun treatment.) Profoundly moved by the result of my amateur attempt at music therapy, I resolved to find out how and why music has such tremendous power. For seven years as a Kindermusik educator and children's music director, I had taught hundreds of children and their families about the joys of music making. We sang, danced, and moved with delight. We rocked the babies and taught the toddlers how to crawl through hoops. We learned to take turns and keep a steady beat. We played musical games and enjoyed old-fashioned circle dances. The parents had fun and noticed the growth and development of their children. The children enjoyed the time with their parents and couldn't wait to come to class and see what was on the agenda for the day. It was thrilling to witness the power of music in this way, but I couldn't help wondering what my next step might be. Was there something more I could do to have a positive impact on people through music? And if music can make such a difference in well children, can it be even more beneficial to the ill or disabled?

I contacted the music therapy program at Marylhurst University, and the rest, as they say, is history. I studied music therapy there for two years, and following the completion of my academic requirements toward the bachelor of music therapy degree, I was accepted as an intern at Portland's Earthtones Music Therapy Services. Earthtones provided me with an extensive clinical background in music therapy with clients with various levels of functioning and therapeutic needs.

*Anne Vitort is the owner of Upbeat Music Therapy Services, LLC and is employed by Seasons Hospice Organization in Portland, Oregon.*

## My Path to Music Therapy
## Emily Wiggins, MT-BC

The years of young single adulthood are the crossroads of life. Depending on the decisions we make, our life could go in virtually any direction. Thus, for several years I've been thinking about what I want to do with life. Fresh out of high school, my perspective was "what can

I possibly do?" which naturally led me to music performance. Music has always been a dominant part of my family's life and mine. So out of the categories available to me, in my mind's eye, performance was the way to go.

Music education to me meant band teacher, and I definitely did not want to be teaching in our public schools—and any private teaching I would do wouldn't necessarily require a degree. It seemed uncanny for me to study composition, as it seemed to necessitate inspiration more than education. Although I'd heard of music therapy at the time, the concept hadn't assimilated itself into my brain yet, and it wasn't available for study at BYU where I was anyways. Music performance hit the closest to the target, and I entered that program. It didn't take too long in the program for me to realize that music performance, although hitting the target, was not the bull's-eye. After dropping out of the program, I explored several other things I could do with my life. I thought about deaf education (being hearing impaired), I thought about special education, and I explored any major available at BYU, and discovered that none was making its mark.

Then I thought about music therapy. At that point in my life, my understanding of the field was extremely limited, knowing nothing about it except its very existence. Life at that time paused as far as college education goes, as I took time off to serve God through my church. All through that time, music therapy was an echo in the back of my mind that grew stronger the more I entertained the possibility. The closer the time came to return to school, the more intriguing music therapy as a field was to me. I knew enough about myself to know that music is such an integrated principle for me that it must be incorporated in my life as more than a side note. I also knew that I held a deep desire to do something in my life that would sincerely mean something to others and me. Thus, I further entertained the idea of music therapy. Through study and prayerful consideration, I eventually came to know that music therapy was the bull's-eye of the target for me. It's an extremely intriguing field, using music as a form of healing and therapy. I'm most fascinated by its effects on children with developmental disabilities. As I had a few handicaps to overcome in life, I'm of the firm belief that handicaps do not have to be disabling. Success can come any way we want it to, and I want to help others learn that principle for themselves. *Emily Wiggins, MT-BC, is the executive director of Dynamic Music Therapy in Las Vegas, Nevada.*

# Chapter 5: What Is a Typical Music Therapy Session?

Like my colleagues, I am often asked to describe a typical music therapy session. I find this to be a difficult question to answer because there is no typical music therapy session! Each session is unique, with specific objectives that are developed as part of a treatment plan. The treatment plan is developed from information gleaned from an assessment. The assessment is a process of evaluating areas of functioning or "domains." These domains are communicative, emotional, social, cognitive or academic, physical or motor, sensory, and often times spiritual. Based on the results of the assessment, a treatment plan is designed that includes specific goals.

## Research

It is critical to highlight the necessity of research in designing a music therapy session. In other words, the music therapist conceives of a plan of action for a session based on results that have been reported in the journals of music therapy. Sometimes periodical references from other health professions will also contribute to a music therapist's knowledge base in planning a session. The wisdom of consulting the research in planning a session enables the music therapist to implement a session from both the scientific and artistic perspective. Thus, music therapy joins science and art. Most importantly, leaning on the research in session planning allows the music therapist to explain to others what occurs in the session via the scientific lens. Research and musical artistry provide the guiding light for all music therapy interventions. The integration of the music therapist's clinical expertise with a research base, addressing the specific needs of the client, results in evidence-based practice.

## Music Therapy with Older Adults

When working with older adults in a senior citizen facility, my first task is to determine the challenges of the residents. These may include physical and sensory issues, intellectual handicaps, memory difficulties leading to and inclusive of dementia of the Alzheimer's type, emotional or mental concerns, and voice problems. This is extremely helpful information, and it may not always be available unless I do an assessment of the group with the facility's staff.

An opening song that lends itself to repeating the residents' names begins the session. This offers a glimpse into the minds and hearts of people who are often hungry for engagement with anyone from the "outside world" in which they no longer fit. Perhaps I'll offer a handshake, and if it is reciprocated, this will tell me about the person's openness to touch and willingness to engage with me as their music therapist. Perhaps music therapy is new to many if not all of the residents, so I like to make the clients comfortable as we meet and greet one another within a song. I have a session plan in mind that will satisfy the objectives of the assessment process for the residents, but it's important to be flexible and ready to respond to the client's responses to the music. I usually allow fifty to fifty-five minutes for such a session.

From an opening "hello song," as we call it, I move on to a rhythmic musical experience using the rhythm instruments in my toolkit: maracas, tambourines, egg shakers, and small drums. I introduce this second musical experience by saying, "I'd love to have you join me. Please feel comfortable playing along with an instrument or simply watching and enjoying the sound." This eliminates any pressure of having to "do something" that may lead to uncomfortable feelings. I proceed with a blues riff, a strong, rhythmic strum on my guitar or the piano, and a statement such as, "Let's move the blues on their way as we begin our new day and play and make music together!"

I watch the music take over as the clients respond by moving and tapping their feet. Their faces come alive as they awaken to the joyful play of making music together! With no rehearsal and possibly no music experience, they coalesce into an ensemble using the rhythm instruments provided. There may be some resistance from some of the residents, and I let them know that it is okay. Just by being there, I know they will reap the untold benefits of the music.

The tempo of this rhythm experience may be one where a quarter note equals seventy-five to ninety beats, depending on the group. The tempo may begin slower, often becoming faster as the experience continues. I move around and give the individuals an opportunity to play louder on their instrument while the rest of the group plays softer. This gives the individual the chance to "shine" and become the leader of this band if they want to participate in this way.

If possible, I have the residents sit in a circle or a half circle, which allows me to move around and approach everyone individually. I collect the rhythm instruments and play a soothing arpeggio on the guitar, always watching to see the people who are looking to me for comforting, musical care. I want to be sure that the music is working for them. I determine on the spot whether to continue the musical engagement using scarves to provoke movement and interaction with each other. We might use slow armchair tai chi movements to call to mind the breath.

We close with a relaxation experience, using recorded music or slow piano music if a piano is available. I use minimal words to invite the group to settle, relax, and be wherever they are in their day.

Depending on the group, I then sing, perhaps without any instrumental accompaniment, a "so long" song such as "Till We Meet Again." I may not address everyone individually with this singing goodbye; it depends on the flow of the group.

## Music Therapy with Special Needs Children

I had thirty-minute music therapy sessions with a special needs child who was five years old. This client had many months of interaction with me, and the assessment took place months ago. The clinical goals have been adjusted over the months to account for her progress and quality of life. Together with her parents, we decided that the primary goals are music making, enjoying music in its various forms, and increasing speech ability.

I conduct the sessions in the family's living room. When I arrive, the child is excited to see me and immediately begins to unpack the bags I am carrying; these hold rhythm instruments, gathering drum, bell chimes, scarves, puppets, and hardbound books. The energy begins to emanate from her first beat on the drum and then the next and the next. Both hands are tapping and pounding, releasing pent-up energy, while she is looking at me, smiling hugely, and sometimes vocalizing "AWwwww." She seems to be experiencing joy as she is allowed to experience all of the instruments in the order she has decided. This "client-led" music therapy is inspiring for me.

Because I'm trying to encourage speech through music, I support all the vocalizations she makes. I consulted with a speech therapist and was given some strategies, and these include sounds and vocalizations that would be good to emphasize through song. They are incorporated in the sessions when possible. As we read from a book that shows pictures of farm animals, the picture of a sheep provokes a "baaaa" from her, and I repeat the sound. When she sees a picture of a dog, a loud "woof" bursts from her, and we "woof woof" together. We play Hide and Seek with the scarves, and when we play Peek-a-Boo, she says *eek-a-boo*—this alerts me to emphasize the *P* sound in future sessions. In a session with one so young and dealing with the challenges unique to her, sometimes twenty to thirty seconds on one of the experiences I've planned is long enough. "When You're Happy and You Know It" has become one of several "touchtone" songs we do together.

Drumming together on the gathering drum provides the transition from one activity to another. I attempt to have a quieting moment toward the close of the session.

Looking at the picture books and playing with colored scarves often takes place toward the end of the session. Such is the flow of a session that is improvisatory but includes clinical objectives and intentions to show observable progress over weeks and months.

## Music Therapy with Veterans

I had the privilege to work with veterans at the VA Medical Center in Milwaukee, Wisconsin, for six and a half years.

One of the formats that brought the veterans joy was a songwriting session to create a theme song for the unit where they resided. Because these veterans all loved music and were musical themselves, to prompt such a creative music experience for them was a joy.

We began a songwriting session with songs they loved while I accompanied them on piano or guitar. Songs such as "Swing Low, Sweet Chariot," "Down by the Riverside," the "Amen" chant, "Lean On Me," and "Home on the Range" worked well for the warm up. We then launched into substituting words for one of the songs and began writing down words based on feelings that they wanted to include in what we call the "parodied song." I might lay down a rhythm progression on the piano or guitar, they shouted out the words they were thinking, and we continued singing melodic variations to go with the chords I played. I often gave them melodic suggestions, and they had the option of saying yes or no.

A session such as this lasted fifty minutes and ended with everyone singing one of his or her favorite songs together. Because I had provided them with a songbook of their requests, it made it easy to jointly decide on a closing song for the session.

There are hundreds of examples of music therapy sessions, and no session is "typical." I hope this gives you an idea of how we work and how creative the work of a music therapist is. Flexibility, creativity, clinical and musical astuteness, caring, compassion, and being in the moment—to enable the best practice and support the clients on their journey—are a few characteristics of the practicing music therapist. What a joy to wake up each morning and say, "I'm a music therapist. How can I serve your needs?"

# Chapter 6: Music Therapy Practice Internationally

The number of music therapists worldwide is in the range of seventeen to eighteen thousand. In the United States, we number around six thousand. Contrast this figure to the 317 million people in the United States and the thirty-five million Canadian inhabitants. Is it any wonder that music therapy is a relatively unknown profession on our continent or throughout the world?

The World Federation of Music Therapy (WFMT) was founded in 1985 in Genoa, Italy. It oversees development of music therapy worldwide and is comprised of eight regions: Africa, Australia/ New Zealand, North America, Latin America, Southeast Asia, Europe, Eastern Mediterranean, and Western Pacific. The WFMT is "dedicated to developing and promoting music therapy throughout the world as an art and a science. The Federation supports the global development of educational programs, clinical practice, and research to demonstrate the contributions of music therapy to humanity."[7] See www.musictherapyworld.net and www.musictherapyworld.net for more information.

It is exciting and a privilege to attend a World Congress hosted by the WFMT. To meet music therapists from all over the world and share strategies is, in the words of the participants, "exhilarating," "energizing," and "amazing." I've had the joy of presenting at several World Congresses over the past years. The financial reality of attending such events makes it cost prohibitive to many music therapists. The good news is that thanks to the Internet, we have access to information about world events in our profession. This brings the global community to our doorstep; the information flows through blogs, websites, and email. How awesome to be connected to our global community!

Since the early 1990s, individual music therapists have enjoyed the support of friends in the music business. Because music therapists needs a variety of instruments in clinical settings and because of the increasing numbers of music therapists, entrepreneurs such as Belli Remo of REMO Music in California and Steve West, founder of WEST Music in Iowa, have become supporters.

The National Association of Music Merchants (NAMM) Foundation and the Support Music Coalition division of NAMM unite nonprofit organizations, schools, and businesses that are working to keep music education strong in their communities.[8]

The GRAMMY Foundation has enthusiastically endorsed our profession. Michael Green, the former president of the foundation, gave an overwhelmingly supportive keynote speech at the AMTA national conference in the early 1990s. He stated that the profession could anticipate an "explosion" in the coming years as the benefits of music therapy became clear to employers, agencies, and institutions. Because many of our professionals possess outstanding prowess on their instruments, the community of music therapy professionals benefits from the notoriety of our colleagues.

# Chapter 7: What Is the Future of Music Therapy?

Although our numbers are small in comparison to the other allied health professions, the employment opportunities for music therapists are growing. Russell Hilliard, PhD, LCSW, LCAT, MT-BC, is the national director of supportive care, research, and ethics for Seasons Hospice and Palliative Care. Hilliard offers an abundance of opportunities for music therapists within his organization, as Seasons Hospice spans seventeen states and provides opportunities for music therapists throughout the country.[9]

As a direct result of the aging US population, the forecast that music therapy will continue to grow is strong. As mentioned in the previous chapter, Michael Green, former president of the GRAMMY Foundation and CEO of the National Academy of Recording Arts and Sciences (NARAS) believes that we could see an "explosion" in the profession. At the 1997 GRAMMY Awards, Green said, "When we look at the body of evidence that the arts contribute to our society, it's absolutely astounding. Music therapists are breaking down the walls of silence and affliction of autism, Alzheimer's, and Parkinson's disease."[10] This is no longer a prediction; it is happening.

## Research

A growing body of research has become available surrounding music therapy practices. The AMTA journals *Music Therapy Perspectives* and *Journal of Music Therapy* routinely report research investigations through both quantitative and qualitative lenses. The Canadian *Journal of Music Therapy* provides accomplishments in the profession from our neighbors to the north. The Nordic *Journal of Music Therapy* serves our international community, and it reports on music therapy procedures and research demonstrations occurring around the globe.

The International Association for Music and Medicine publishes the interdisciplinary journal, *Music and Medicine*. It provides "an integrative forum for clinical practice and research related to music interventions and applications of clinical music strategies in medicine."[11]

The research reported in these journals shines the spotlight on the clinical experiences of a music therapist's work. The reports garner the attention of the medical and scientific arenas and positively impact job creation.

## Music Therapy in the News

In May 2011, Dr. Sanjay Gupta of CNN tweeted, "Music therapy helps speech, but also motor skills, memory and balance. Also emotionally uplifting."[12] Another well-known physician, Oliver Sacks, reported that patients with neurological disorders who cannot talk or move are often able to sing, sometimes even dance, to music. Sacks may be better known from the movie *Awakenings*, a must see for anyone interested in learning about music therapy's effect on people suffering from a neurological disease.

Advocates say that "music therapy also can help ease the trauma of grieving, lessen depression, and provide an outlet for people who are otherwise withdrawn."[13]

Senator Harry Reid stated, "Music therapy is much more complicated than playing records in nursing homes. Therapists are trained in psychology, group interaction, and the special needs of the elderly."[14]

## The Future

We may be rightfully convinced about the positive future for the profession of music therapy. Today's music therapists are reaping the rewards of the work of the many talented professionals who have gone before us. Their creative contributions have helped to move the profession forward so that we can help people who need our services.

There is little question that as the word spreads about what we do and how we use music in our work, job openings will occur. As music therapists become more available, the general populace will reap the benefits from our professional services through the music of their choice.

## Closing Remarks

It is my hope that through the voices and words of my colleagues' essays, others may be inspired to consider becoming a music therapist. While the acceptance and need for our services is steadily increasing, it is necessary to highlight the ongoing need to educate the public about who we are, what we do, how we do it, and where we work. The fact that we are still so few in number (compared to the rest of the population) amplifies the fact that there's always going to be work involved in getting the word out and not enough of us to do the work.

There is little doubt that music therapy as a profession inspires joy for both the client and the therapist. Viva la musica!

# Notes

1. Judith Egerton, "Medical Musicality," *Louisville Magazine,* http://loumag.epubxp.com/i/53439/40.

2. American Music Therapy Association, http://www.musictherapy.org.

3. Michael Thaut, "A New Challenge for Music Therapy: The Correctional Setting," *Music Therapy Perspectives* 4 (1987): 44–50.

4. Center for Biomedical Research in Music, http://www.cbrm.colostate.edu/research/ongoing-projects.

5. Barbara Reuer, Resounding Joy, http://www.resoundingjoyinc.org.

6. Home Youth and Resource Center, http://www.homeyouthcenter.org.

7. The World Federation of Music Therapy, http://www.musictherapyworld.net/WFMT/Home.

8. National Association of Music Merchants, http://www.namm.org.

9. Seasons Hospice and Palliative Care, http://www.seasons.org.

10. American Music Therapy Association, http://www.musictherapy.org/quotes.

11. International Association for Music and Medicine, http://www.iammonline.com.

12. American Music Therapy Association, http://www.musictherapy.org/quotes.

13. American Music Therapy Association, http://www.musictherapy.org/quotes.

14. American Music Therapy Association, http://www.musictherapy.org/quotes.

# Further Resources

*An Introduction to Music Therapy: Theory and Practice* by William Davis, Michael Thaut, and Kate Gfeller

Certification Board for Music Therapists
www.cbmt.org/examination/get-certified

Canadian Association for Music Therapy
www.musictherapy.ca/en

*Nordic Journal of Music Therapy*
http://www.tandfonline.com/toc/rnjm20/current#

*British Journal of Music Therapy*
http://www.bamt.org/british-association-for-music-therapy-resources/journal.html

# About the Author

Christine Korb, MM, MT-BC, director of music therapy at Pacific University, has made a significant contribution in the world of music and music therapy. In addition to many years of clinical experience, she has experience as a composer, author, researcher, book reviewer, and presenter. She has presented at various American Music Therapy Association Conferences, the 2002 World Federation of Music Therapy Conference in Oxford, the Healing Symposium of the Fairbanks Summer Arts Festival in 2004, and the World Federation of Music Therapy Conference in Buenos Aires in 2008. She is a frequent book reviewer for the journal *The Arts in Psychotherapy*.

Her research on dementia of the Alzheimer's type appears in the 1997 *Canadian Journal of Music Therapy*. She received a grant from the Helen Bader Foundation to conduct this research while employed at the VA Medical Center in Milwaukee, Wisconsin.

She is the author of the rhythm-based violence prevention project for children, The Drum Trail Project. Her current research, The Soul Song Project, is a ten-year longitudinal investigation to determine the effects of singing in choirs on participants' mood, stress, and energy levels.

She has written many children's and folk songs, including the published choral work for women's voices, "Namaste," which premiered in Poland. A trip to Brazil's Amazon River inspired her instrumental ensemble piece, "Dusk on the Amazon," in which instruments imitate the animal and bird sounds emanating from this rich and endangered territory.

Because teaching future music therapists has become her way of life during the past sixteen years, Chris no longer composes or writes as frequently—her students have become her compositions in real time. She is grateful and continually inspired to do the work of a music therapist and educator.